A PRACTICAL
TO HELPING CHILDREN AND YOUNG PEOPLE WHO EXPERIENCE TRAUMA

Panos Vostanis

Speechmark

To Kenzy, a little boy who loved life

First published in 2016 by
Speechmark Publishing Ltd,
2nd Floor, 5 Thomas More Square, London E1W 1YW, UK
Tel: +44 (0)845 034 4610; Fax: +44 (0)845 034 4649
www.speechmark.net

Design and artwork by Moo Creative (Luton)

002-5996/Printed in the United Kingdom by CMP (uk) Ltd

British Library Cataloguing in Publication Data
A catalogue record for this book is available from the British Library

ISBN 978 1 90930 135 1

Acknowledgements

To all the children and young people whose strength I have been privileged to share over the years.

Preface

Children and young people who experience traumatic events in their early lives often have multiple needs and are disadvantaged by not properly accessing mainstream services. Despite the challenges that they pose, the way we approach them individually and organisationally is the ultimate marker of values by services and societies alike. Why, after all, do children who are most in need tend to receive so little?

Despite a number of barriers, our knowledge, evidence and examples of good practice increase all the time. I tried to view children through the lenses of carers, teachers, people working in social care or other youth practitioners who I was privileged to know and work with over the years. Everyone has a role to play within their agency remit and professional or carer role, hence my attempt to highlight both interventions and service models that can best meet vulnerable children's needs.

Contents

Chapter 1

Impact of trauma on children

Psychological trauma

Psychological trauma can be acute or chronic; it can be the case of a single event (such as an accident or natural disaster) or it can occur through a chain of multiple and interrelated incidents – often referred to as complex trauma, like abuse in the context of domestic violence and family breakdown. All traumatic events will cause distress in children, and a high proportion of traumatic events will lead to child mental health problems. Trauma has a cumulative effect, that is, the more exposed a child is to similar events, the more vulnerable to or at risk of suffering from ill mental health the child will be. The mechanisms can be direct, such as from experiencing and witnessing violence, or they can be indirect, through lack of safety or impaired parenting capacity. Trauma impacts on most aspects of a child's life, hence the relevance of this text to all carers and professionals in contact with children and young people (hereafter mostly referred to in the text as simply 'children', although both terms will be used intermittently).

Some children are particularly vulnerable

The interplay between different types of trauma and exposure over a number of years means that certain young groups are particularly vulnerable to experiencing psychological trauma, and these groups will thus form the focus of this handbook. It, however, needs to be acknowledged that these often overlap. Young groups who are particularly vulnerable include:

- children and young people in public care (fostering, kinship care or in residential homes)
- children who have been adopted
- homeless children and families – usually victims of domestic violence
- single homeless young people
- asylum-seeking and refugee children (and their parents)
- unaccompanied minors
- juvenile offenders.

Child development from a trauma perspective

It is always useful to have a good understanding of different theories when working with any child, as this will provide a framework to formulate their difficulties before tailoring an intervention. In the case of traumatised children this is even more important, as there may be limited or fragmented information on their early life, their presentations can be perplexing and their environmental adversities may be pretty overwhelming. Such theories to take into consideration, and that are not mutually exclusive in planning interventions, are broadly driven by:

- *cognitive and social approaches,* like Piaget's cognitive stages, Vygotsky's complex thinking patterns, Erikson's psychosocial development, Kohlberg's moral development, and social empathy (theory of mind)
- *emotion-focused or psychodynamic,* from Freud's early psychosexual stages, Vaillant's defence mechanisms or Winnicott's object relations theories
- *attachment-based,* mainly from Bowlby's pioneering work, and followed by the definition of attachment styles from Ainsworth and Main.

Exercise

Consider this child's needs from different developmental perspectives. How is her emotional, cognitive and social development likely to differ from a child of the same chronological age who has not had similar traumatic experiences?

Lucy is seven years of age. Along with her three younger siblings, from birth she suffered severe abuse and neglect. The children were left unattended, starving and dirty for days. Lucy tried to look after her siblings as well as she could, and she missed most of her first year at school. Her mother was either out or exhausted in bed from drug use. Several partners came and went over the years. The neighbours called social services on several occasions, who tried to help Lucy's mum with family and practical support and respite care. These measures only worked for short periods, however. When two toddlers from the home were found wandering in the street, all four children were removed to foster care. Unfortunately for Lucy, she had to be placed separately from her siblings. She has been in this placement for 18 months, and she is likely to remain there in the long term.

Lucy does not cause any trouble at home. She sits quietly for hours and plays with toys but cannot yet follow games rules, no matter how much she is prompted. Sometimes she looks sad during the day and sometimes she sobs in her sleep. She seems pleased to see her siblings once a fortnight, but she does not know what activities to engage in with them. At school, her reading and writing have come along, but she drifts between children in the playground and has no friends.

Case scenario

Now revisit Lucy's case from those developmental perspectives. How can your previous formulation inform ways of helping Lucy at this stage of her life?

- *Emotional development:* Lucy seems to hold back and not express or process her emotions. This is not surprising; after all this is how she survived over the years. If she cried or protested, she was probably told off or hit. Both her carers and teachers need to model a different and more nurturing approach, while remaining mindful of Lucy's history and appreciating that it will take some time before she spontaneously expresses her feelings. They may need to spell those out as if she were a younger child. Life-story work could help Lucy make sense of her experiences. Whether she needs more specialist psychotherapeutic input will depend on the above steps and her responses.

- *Psychosocial development:* Similarly, Lucy cannot spontaneously relate to other children. There is a danger that the gap with her peers may widen without help, and even lead to secondary problems such as aggression. Here, Lucy will need a mixed approach of supervision, direction and safe experimentation until she can handle relationships on her own. On some occasions she should be treated like a younger child, but her carers must keep prompting her by making social activities more demanding.

- *Cognitive development:* There are promising signs that Lucy can learn and make up for her lost schooling. She is likely, however, to require a personalised educational plan, tailored strategies and individual teacher time for a while. The key risk is the social side of her school attendance, that is, whether her social deficits can hinder her learning. For this reason, tackling both domains should be a priority.

- *Attachment relationships:* Lucy is tentative, to say the least, in trusting adults – and why should she? Her foster carers need to gradually and patiently bring her into their family by regaining her trust. To do so, they will require their own support and will need to manage their expectations, as Lucy may not be able to give back her affection for a while. Additional measures, such as attending a foster carers group or therapeutic input involving the carers (for example, theraplay), may be necessary if the previous steps have not been enough.

This could highlight the importance of a child's emotions, behaviours, cognitions, attachments and peer relationships and integrate these. We could draw Lucy in the centre of a page, with five bubbles of Lucy in those five domains (emotions, behaviours, cognitions, attachments and peer relationships) around her.

In conclusion, all developmental theories are important, and they are no longer considered mutually exclusive in understanding children who suffered trauma. Their knowledge can help a carer or practitioner to:

- observe and interpret behaviours and needs from different perspectives
- avoid enmeshment and confusion of complex presentations
- choose an intervention that will be best matched to the child's needs and wishes
- remain clear on both the indications and limitations of this intervention.

Factors that make children vulnerable

What children carry from birth and experience onwards will invariably influence how they grow up and function. Although some factors that place them at risk of developing and sustaining mental health problems are obvious, it is worth adopting a more systematic approach to risk factors by considering the following:

- It is important to consider the cumulative effects of risk factors, that is, the more of them that there are and/or the longer they go on for, the more adverse will be their impact.
- While bearing the above in mind, it is important to recognise that risk factors are neither critical nor irreversible.
- One should consider that risk factors are often interrelated, and one can lead to another.
- It is important to think about the fact that risk factors may predispose a child to a problem or precipitate an episode.
- It is important to think about the fact that risk factors can have a direct or indirect effect on a child.

Child vulnerabilities

Risk or vulnerability factors can be related to the child, their family, the school(s) they attend and their and wider community.

Individual factors

- Temperamental traits
- Genetic susceptibility
- Prenatal or perinatal
- Physical ill health

Within the family

- Family conflict
- Domestic violence
- Abuse and neglect
- Negative or inconsistent parenting
- Parental mental illness or drug use

At school and in the community

- Bullying
- Exposure to violence
- Peer pressure
- Lack of social and attainment opportunities
- Being unsafe
- Discrimination
- Social and school exclusion

Protective and resilience factors

Protective and resilience factors constantly try to compensate for adversity and can be a source of hope, even under very difficult circumstances. Protective factors fall under the same domains as risk factors:

Individual

- Ability to learn, process and reflect on new information
- Adaptability
- Self-regulation
- Sense of cultural identity and belonging
- Self-worth and confidence

Family related

- Secure attachment
- Nurturing and affection
- Consistent and firm parenting
- Role models

At school and in the community

- Friendships
- Attainment and sense of achievement
- Support networks
- Community safety

Exercise

Think of a needy and vulnerable child under your care. Try to formulate vulnerability and protective factors under the previous framework.

Case scenario

How would you minimise the risk factors and maximise the protective ones in this difficult situation?

Jonathan is 15 and has just come out of a secure institution, following a violent attack on another young man. His dad told me that he will kick Jonathan out if he gets into any more trouble. As a matter of fact, his dad has kicked him loads of times in the past. Jonathan can hardly read – what's the point of going back to school? He gets a break when he smokes whiff – but he no longer has the money. He likes boxing, although he tends to lose interest. He already hates himself – 'they must have been taking the mickey' in prison when they told him he had a good voice.

Chapter 2

Mental health concerns, problems and differences from other children

Transient or impairing problems

Knowing when to seek help for a child's mental health is not always a straightforward decision. Many isolated symptoms like nightmares or oppositional behaviours will settle over time with reassurance and simple techniques such as behavioural charts. When a few of those problems persevere and begin to impact on the child's life, carers and professionals involved need to keep a close eye on the child and consider strategies, often in coordination between home and school. If none of these work and the problems become more severe and entrenched, that is, moving into the sphere of 'disorder' or 'impairment', an external opinion and possibly input would be appropriate.

Why it is particularly difficult for traumatised children to seek help

- Their mental health is masked by environmental changes and other social care difficulties.
- They often move between placements and carers.
- Different practitioners hold different pieces of information, which are not corroborated and can even be conflicting.
- Their primary carer is typically weakened in their parenting capacity, and struggling with their own distress and needs.
- Little is typically known about the early history of traumatised children, with other gaps in their development.
- They find it difficult to engage with agencies.
- They cannot distinguish between therapeutic agencies and statutory agencies that may reinforce their fear of being taken away.

Why mainstream services can often not cater as well for this youth group

- Mainstream services are primarily designed for children and families living in relative stability.
- The entry routes (care pathways) of mainstream services make 'stability' assumptions, for example, that the child is registered with or will visit a family doctor to instigate a referral or that the child attends school.

- Consequently, they assume that the primary caregiver will advocate for the child.
- They have loose but not systematic links with key agencies, or settings like children's homes and hostels.
- Staff may have good clinical skills, but they are not necessarily geared towards children who suffered substantial abuse and neglect, and their carers.
- They may simply not have adequate resources, including time, for a holistic and more preventive, rather than crisis-driven, approach.
- Overall, they are not tailored to these children's needs – for example, for the particular needs of homeless children.

Types of common child mental health problems

- Overall, one in ten children suffers from mental health problems of sufficient severity and distress to merit assessment and external help.
- This rate rises with deprivation and exposure to risk factors such as trauma.
- For example, children in care have four to five times a higher chance of developing mental health problems than the average child.
- In reality, it is unlikely that most of those problems will be recognised and, if so, that children will be able to access appropriate services.
- Therefore, it is even more important to maximise all available types of help, particularly for less severe and complex difficulties, through continual staff training, direct links and access to specialist services and establishment of care pathways.
- Children exposed to trauma and other adversities are more likely to have more than one mental health problem (for example, aggression, self-harm and depression).
- Mental health problems can overlap or appear similar, and hence it can be difficult to distinguish between them. For example, hyper-arousal because of trauma and attachment difficulties is similar to hyperactivity because of a neurodevelopmental condition such as attention deficit hyperactivity disorder (ADHD).
- These may continue in later life without intervention, become entrenched or even get worse as additional or secondary vulnerabilities occur (for example, drug use, poverty and/or abuse after living on the street).

Emotional problems include various anxiety types (including generalised, social, phobic and obsessive-compulsive), depression and posttraumatic stress reactions. Overall, they affect about 4 per cent of the general population (but multiplied in the face of adversity). Typical presentations include:

- *generalised anxiety*: excessive worries (thoughts) and physical complaints (such as aches, sweating, nausea, sickness, palpitations and muscular tension) and sleep disturbance
- *social anxiety*: persistent and irrational fears of social situations, with associated anxiety symptoms, and avoidance
- *phobias*: persistent and irrational fears of specific objects (such as certain animals or the dark) or particular situations
- *obsessive-compulsive*: intrusive and distressing thoughts, resistance but awareness (in contrast with psychosis), urges for unacceptable acts (for example, touching) or thoughts (for example, swearing), compulsion to repeat acts (such as hand washing)
- *depression*: expressed as, for instance, pervasive low mood, irritability, negative cognitions such as guilt or self-blame, loss of appetite and weight (sometimes overeating), feeling tired, loss of interest, withdrawal, sleep difficulties, difficulty concentrating and self-harm thoughts or acts
- *posttraumatic stress*: reliving the trauma through thoughts, images or nightmares; avoiding reminders of trauma such as certain places or situations; and arousal, including hyper-vigilance.

Self-reflection

Consider the pros and cons of using the term 'posttraumatic stress disorder' (PTSD):

- Are we pathologising what is essentially a normal human response to adverse experiences?
- Alternatively, are we minimising children's distress, thus depriving them of help?
- Or, does it not matter what we call it but rather what we choose to do?
- Which factors should influence our judgements and decisions?
- What is the evidence for or against our beliefs?

Behavioural problems are heterogeneous in their underlying causes and presentations. They are present in about 5 per cent of the general population, and they co-occur with most emotional and neurodevelopmental problems, which can mask the real picture. There is an ongoing debate about whether these constitute mental health problems as such, and which agency is predominantly responsible. Understanding their nature is the first step in deciding the best way to help, as it is likely that all adults in contact with the child will need to adopt a consistent approach. One can crudely distinguish between three types:

- *oppositional* (argumentativeness, temper tantrums, anger and defiance): due to inconsistent discipline and parenting strategies, and that should be interpreted according to the child's chronological and developmental age, as the two may not be the same
- *conduct* (more severe aggression, violence, stealing, lying and truanting): also related to lack of boundaries, but compounded by exposure to violence at home and in the community through their peer group
- *attachment* (emotional dysregulation, including angry outbursts): primarily due to abuse and neglect, but compounded by moves and multiple placements/carers. The terms 'attachment types', 'attachment difficulties' or 'attachment disorders' are used variably, with lack of agreement between the classification systems on their specific characteristics. Traumatised children often present with reactive attachment of either the inhibited type (inability to initiate or sustain social interactions) or the disinhibited type (misinterpreting social cues for affection). Both types can be difficult to differentiate from neurodevelopmental deficits related to the next group.

Neurodevelopmental conditions typically include attention deficit hyperactivity disorder (ADHD) and autism spectrum disorders (ASD), and imply a neurobiological cause, although research findings are inconclusive on the specific mechanisms. Their threshold has been lowered in recent years, meaning better recognition, but also the need for services and evidence-based information. Both disorders and related deficits are particularly common among vulnerable children, maybe because of sharing common risk factors in early childhood or even earlier. The key difficulty is in distinguishing from environmentally related attachment difficulties because of (at least superficially) similar presentations. These can be determined with a thorough assessment, including observation and a school visit and/or school report, but this may not be entirely possible at the beginning of the placement (for example, when adopted), as these features may become more prominent when the child has settled in a safe environment. The lack of information on their early development is also a constraint, particularly for the diagnosis of ASD. Key features to look out for for ADHD and the autism spectrum, respectively, are:

- *ADHD:* physical overactivity or restlessness; impaired capacity to concentrate, register new information or remain on task; and impulsivity, accounting for the child's age
- *autism spectrum:* variable degree of difficulty in understanding social behaviours, lack of social empathy, restricted or narrow interests, impaired verbal and non-verbal communication and resistance to change (the latter being an example commonly seen, for different reasons, in children with attachment difficulties).

Exercise

You are a teacher at a mainstream primary school. Becky is six. She was adopted almost two years ago. Her parents 'love her to bits', but she is a handful. She does not easily settle, moving from one task to another, and she is beginning to annoy the other children who attend the same school as her, who are nevertheless fond of her. She seems bright enough, although she is constantly losing ground in the classroom. Becky wants to please but does not seem to know how. She can quickly blow if things do not go her way, only to then say how sorry she is. At the recent parents' evening, her dad thought that this is normal 'after what she went through', while her mum wondered if 'something is wrong' with Becky that they were not told about. Your colleagues are equally split. Some encourage you to nurture her as she will 'grow out of it', while others advocate that Becky would be better suited to attendance at a special needs school.

- What would you consider as potential explanations for Becky's difficulties?
- What internal steps would you take to help Becky within the school?
- How would you be liaising with and working with the family?
- When and why would you be seeking input from an external agency?

Other problems, predominantly during adolescence, include early onset of mental illness and eating disorders:

- *Psychosis* includes abnormal perceptual phenomena (hallucinations) and ideas (delusions), which may indicate early onset of schizophrenia, brief drug-related episodes or bipolar affective disorder with significant mood fluctuations. Typical symptoms may not develop for a while, instead starting with gradual changes such as social withdrawal and out-of-character behaviours. Young people who suffered trauma can experience abnormal perceptions such as hearing voices, but these are usually in the context of their past experiences. The child becomes troubled while maintaining a sense of their unreal nature (in contrast with psychosis, when the young person is convinced that what they experience is real).

- *Eating disorders* broadly include *anorexia* and *bulimia nervosa*. They can present with different levels of severity, and can start in childhood. Young people with anorexia develop a distorted body image, and lose at least 15 per cent of their expected weight through excessive exercising, dieting and/or self-inducing vomiting. Bulimia is characterised by intermittent binge eating and getting rid of these calories through vomiting, purgatives and/or appetite suppressants.

Case scenario

Billy is 15 and has been living in a foster home for three years. He suffered physical abuse and neglect in earlier life, and was in and out of care until there was enough evidence to remove Billy and his younger brother from their birth family. His stepfather was prosecuted and given a prison sentence, taking into account other offences. This sentence is shortly coming to an end, as Billy recently found out from his aunt, who remains in touch. His school work appears to have been affected, and Billy has been spending increasing time in his bedroom. He is as pleasant as usual, but rather distracted. When his foster carer asked him if anything has been worrying him, Billy replied, 'The voices have been telling him to go and get the ****** [stepfather].'

Question: Could Billy be becoming psychotic?

Considerations of emerging picture: Billy is clearly troubled. It is unlikely that he is developing a psychosis, as his complaints are congruent with a real reminder of past trauma, and therefore the 'voices' are possibly of traumatic nature. In addition to finding ways of relieving Billy's distress and protecting him, there is a risk that he may act on his 'voices' (or thoughts), whatever their real cause. An emerging psychosis would probably be accompanied by other changes and deterioration in his social and school functioning, which are worth looking out for, no matter how implausible this seems at this point. Without panicking, one could bear in mind the small possibility that this real stressor may have triggered a mental episode, even if not causally related. Either way, if these complaints persist after reassurance from his carers and other close adults, the decision to involve an external mental health practitioner could ensure sharing and following up these concerns.

Chapter 3

Interventions: Meeting vulnerable children's needs in the context of one's role

Before deciding the most appropriate way of helping a particular child, it is as important to pose a number of questions:

- What is the theoretical framework of the proposed intervention (also see below) and what are its goals?
- What is the evidence-base for its effectiveness?
- Are the goals realistic for this child in their current living circumstances?
- Is the intervention dependent on other (usually environmental) changes?
- Is it possible to provide the intervention, considering the available skills and resources?
- Is this proposed for positive reasons (because of a good chance that it will work) rather than by default ('nothing else has worked')?
- If it has been tried before, why again? What is different? Why has it not previously worked?
- Are there adjustments or modifications compared to the same intervention for a child living in relative stability?
- Who will provide the intervention? Is the required level matched to this practitioner's role, rather than trying to compensate for a gap elsewhere in the system?
- Has this person got available supports such as training and supervision and is there the time for it to be provided properly?

Main types of therapeutic interventions and how they may differ for vulnerable children

First, it is important to consider some issues related to all children, before contrasting with what may be different for children who suffer trauma. Interventions broadly reflect the developmental theories discussed in the previous chapter. They tend to originate from 'large' therapeutic schools (psychoanalysis, social learning, attachment and systems/cybernetics), which gradually evolved, broke down or were integrated into new modalities (like counselling or cognitive-behavioural therapy) with more recent adaptations to the needs of particular young groups (such as dialectical-behavioural therapy or theraplay). The available evidence is variable in its quality and generalisability. Findings usually originate from 'top-down' research trials, which are in the process of being tested in real life, but are constrained by the nature of this population. In the meanwhile, most new approaches are being applied 'bottom-up', that is, in practice, and with smaller-scale evaluations in clinical or other service settings. Emerging guidelines try to marry the two trends, often relying on expert consensus. This means that we will continue to grapple with this discordance and uncertainty for a while. While we do so, we can still critically question both ends of this debate, that is, that 'it does not matter if there is no evidence, because of the nature of psychological interventions' against 'we need pure evidence before we try out an emerging approach'.

Below, let's consider the key underpinnings and indications of the main therapeutic approaches, in particular by highlighting their challenges and modifications for vulnerable children.

Behavioural therapy

- Behavioural therapy is based on social learning theory.
- Behavioural therapy aims at reinforcing desirable behaviours and outcomes as well as reducing, changing and reframing undesirable ones, for example, sleeping problems, eating problems, phobias, anxiety and/or aggression.
- Behavioural therapy is not concerned with trying to help understand the underlying cause, although links may be made during this process.
- With behavioural therapy it is believed that goals need to be clear, realistic (that is, achievable), consistent and developmentally appropriate – without changing the goals or making them up as one goes along.
- With behavioural therapy it is believed that goals need to be agreed with and clearly communicated to the child and the parents or carers.
- With behavioural therapy it is believed that goals need to be regularly monitored.
- Behavioural therapy is not exclusive from other interventions, but differences should be clearly demarcated.

Applications with vulnerable children

- Behaviours should also be understood in the context of trauma, and hence behavioural strategies may need to be complemented by an attachment-focused intervention, as otherwise they can reinforce previous rejection.

- When applying behavioural therapy with vulnerable children it is important to ensure consistency among multiple carers such as a children's home and the child's school.
- When applying behavioural therapy with vulnerable children it is important to ensure risk reduction and containment/safety, either as a prerequisite or parallel to other, predominantly trauma-focused, interventions.

Cognitive-behavioural therapy (CBT)

- Cognitive-behavioural therapy is based on theory that trauma and abuse lead to negative thinking patterns, which in turn affect feelings and behaviour.
- Cognitive-behavioural therapy aims at challenging and changing negative cognitions such as 'I am to blame' and 'It has always been my fault'.
- Cognitive-behavioural therapy incorporates a variable degree of behavioural tasks, depending on the young person's capacity to process thoughts and/or to complement with behavioural strategies.
- Carers can be involved in reinforcing these goals.
- There is increasing evidence for the effectiveness of cognitive-behavioural therapy, not only for mental health disorders like depression but also for young people who suffered trauma.
- Cognitive-behavioural therapy is not necessarily a specialist approach but requires suitable training.
- Cognitive-behavioural therapy is more suitable for adolescents and young adults, but some older children may have developed cognitive ability to use certain simple strategies.

Applications with vulnerable young people

- Some vulnerable young people may prefer the structure of CBT, although this should not be simplified as CBT 'being easy'.
- Young offenders or male teenagers may find CBT more acceptable than psychodynamic reflective approaches, but this is not a generalisation.
- Young people in turmoil may find it difficult to keep diaries, or they may not even know how to write, so it is believed important with CBT to maintain a flexible style without losing the strengths of the intervention.

- Groups will need suitable preparation to get young people roughly on the same wavelength.
- Tackling cognitions and their links with feelings, young people can easily divert from the therapeutic model, that is, they can shift to psychotherapy 'by default'.

Family therapy (systemic or other frameworks)

- Family therapy involves two individuals, a family, a staff group or a wider unit such as a school as a system that is qualitatively different from the sum of its parts.
- It is understood with family therapy that interactions are essential in the maintenance of this unit, whether these are functional or not.
- This is a useful way of also looking at interactions between subsystems, for example, between the family and the school.
- Typically, family therapy tries to change family communication and relationships.
- Techniques are adapted to this model such as circular questioning that tries to unravel individuals' views of one another's perceptions, and reframing of maladaptive behaviours.

Applications with vulnerable young people

- There needs to be some safe boundaries when applying family therapy with vulnerable young people, for example, a more practical family support period may be indicated first if there is acting out or physical aggression within the session or pronounced similar behaviours between sessions.
- Therapeutic goals need to be clear, and they need to be distinguished from a behavioural or attachment-focused intervention, although some of their techniques can be incorporated.
- The establishment of clear therapeutic goals very much relies on a good assessment, and agreement of goals with the carers and young person.
- Family therapy can be valuable in understanding a staff group such as at a shelter or children's home within consultation.

Attachment-focused interventions

- Attachment-focused interventions are almost exclusively geared towards children with some level of vulnerability, but the extent (severity) of that vulnerability and the particular circumstances will determine the nature of the intervention.

- Although there are similarities with other approaches, like psychodynamic therapy, with attachment-focused interventions goals are defined within the parent (or carer)–child relationship.
- There are different combinations with attachment-focused interventions as new models evolve, for example, seeing the child and then including the parent or carer every few sessions or working jointly throughout or working in parallel.
- It can be applied to staff groups like teachers or children's homes staff, but needs to be adapted to multiple carers rather than as a single carer approach.
- The objectives should be cautiously defined if a child is in transition, for example, if they are to move from the children's home; in such cases, encouraging nurturing rather than a particular attachment relationship may be preferable.

Pharmacological treatment

- The indications of pharmacological treatment should be clearly determined, communicated and agreed with the child in a developmentally appropriate language, and with the parents or carers.
- The potential side effects of pharmacological treatment should also be clearly determined, communicated and agreed with the child in a developmentally appropriate language and with the parents or carers with a monitoring and safety plan on who to contact if there are any concerns.
- On the whole, medication is not the first line of treatment for most child mental health problems (even when dealing with depression or ADHD).
- Children's, parents' and teachers' views should be established at the outset, particularly where disagreements may be likely.
- Explaining what medication is *not* meant to achieve is equally important to its indications.
- Usually, the use of medication should be placed within an overall care plan.

Applications with vulnerable young people

- Both assessment and treatment are likely to be more complex, because of interrelated (mainly attachment) needs that overlap with certain symptoms and the multiple carers involved (with different perceptions, observations and narratives).

- Consistency and corroboration are paramount during the assessment, at its conclusion and throughout medication reviews.
- Safety issues such as the administration and supervision of medication are more prominent for young people living on their own (for example, in hostels) and/or in an unstable environment.
- Indications for the use of medication can be misconstrued, usually as helping with difficult behaviours, and this can be communicated as a veiled threat to the child.

The above list is far from exhaustive, but rather aims to highlight the principles behind the key modalities and how these can be applied with vulnerable children and youth. It is positive that new branches or evolving psychological interventions continually emerge and are subject to evaluation, and practitioners implement them with 'hard-to-reach' groups.

Case scenario

Gale is 15 years, and has recently moved to a children's home following three unsuccessful foster placements. She is pleasant and enjoys being with other residents most of the time. But Gale can also quickly 'fly off the handle'. The slightest request from the staff makes her agitated, following which she tends to storm out. There are times when she will soon return back to 'normal', while on other occasions Gale goes into her room and starts cutting her arms. She will use any sharp object that she can find, no matter how many precautions the staff take. Alternatively, Gale absconds and may not come back for a day or two. Nobody knows where she stays, but there are fears that she may be being sexually exploited. The staff are getting desperate with respect to thinking of ways of how to help Gale. At an urgent review meeting, the suggestion of 'Gemma needing therapy' is put forward to her social worker.

How would you approach this situation, need and request?

First, consider all information, including past history surrounding Gale's abuse and neglect, previous placements, the pattern of her behaviours, her social functioning and her views. Then break down different behaviours or presentations, and consider the rationale, goals and limitations of various therapeutic options. It is unlikely that all will be readily available; Gale may not wish or be able to engage and priorities may need to be set in a sequential or parallel (but certainly integral) care plan. Here are some of these options:

- Behavioural strategies initially help to prevent or minimise risk and gradually, over time, to increase positive behaviours. All staff need to be in agreement and remain consistent, with regular reviews, while involving Gale in each step.
- Strategies in keeping herself safe can be discussed with Gale, and they can be reinforced by staff.
- Individual sessions can help Gale link her emotions and behaviours, before beginning to regulate them such as in the form of dialectical behaviour therapy (DBT).
- If Gemma is settled enough to reflect and appears ready for a psychodynamic approach, this approach could help her to make links with her past trauma over a sustained period.

Chapter 4

Children and young people in foster care

Recognising needs

The circumstances that lead to a placement (emergency or planned) will inevitably colour foster carers' preparation and planning, but they should not compromise the quality of information that the foster carers receive and the support systems that are put in place. Carers should always be clear of the child's history, including past behaviours, particularly if the behaviours led to a placement breakdown at some point. There is no point in hoping that 'things will be OK this time'; try to understand what has worked (or not) before, and thus what to anticipate. It is also tempting to focus on the negatives and forget to establish what the child likes, what are their strengths and what are their areas of interest, which can prove the crucial bridging point in the new placement.

The same applies to other important environments and professionals, notably school and teachers. If the child remains at the same school, this will be their haven and their main chance of continuity, and therefore their life there needs to be protected while teachers remain aware of the difficult changes in their life. Continuity does not mean that everything will go on as usual. How would any one of us feel or perform at work if we did not know where we were going to live, and for how long? If the child has moved to a new school, it can be a hard act to help the child to integrate without feeling 'different', and one needs to remain watchful and ready to step in when necessary. The following scenario can be viewed through different angles, that is, from the foster carers', social worker's, teacher's or youth worker's eyes.

Self-reflection

You are a teacher in a mainstream primary school. Judith is a seven-year-old girl who has just moved from another part of the country to live with a local foster family. You were told that she was 'unmanageable' both at home and at school, and social services have had to look hard to find this 'specialist' foster placement, the third in less than a year for Judith. Your head teacher only knows that she was badly abused before taken into care. She has been in your class for three days so far.

What emotions does Judith evoke in you?

- Fear that follows her history?
- Anxiety because of her unpredictability and the impact she may have on the other children?

- Sympathy for her sad predicament?
- Wish to protect Judith and help turn her life around?
- Resentment because she never smiles back and just stares at you?
- Swinging between not wanting to be seen as either 'soft' or 'harsh'?
- All of the above emotions at different times?

Becoming aware of these feelings is not that different from a therapy interaction, as it mirrors Judith's inner world and the fragmentation of her own emotional self. She also experiences all the above at different times. The difference from her being in therapy is that you must carry on operating in the real world, but also bear in mind the needs of the rest of the classroom, too.

Human responses, teaching style and behavioural strategies are often difficult to disentangle – particularly in the heat of the moment, such as if Judith hits another child, seemingly without provocation. Do you feel comfortable that you can handle difficult situations without additional support for reflection from a colleague?

Recognising early a child's mental health needs

Although one can never extinguish an element of surprise or of the unknown, being well-informed and prepared is essential. If information is not volunteered, this should be actively sought, preferably in a face-to-face meeting with the child's social worker and foster carer *before* she actually starts. Direct feedback on her history, past concerns, developmental capacity and overall profile can be corroborated by access to previous reports and documentation. Having a plan on how to best integrate Judith should include different scenarios, with a tight monitoring process, liaison and communication with her carers and social workers and swift response if need be – without spontaneous reactions if things get worse such as of excluding or removing her prematurely. If there are doubts about the family or school placement, this is the time to say so. It can be much worse if these doubts fester, as the child will sense them and act on them, and the adults will get angry with one another.

In determining whether to be concerned about the child's mental health, written or verbal information from important adults who know the child should ideally be complemented by observations and direct evidence from the child themselves. Some tips relate to all children, but let's predominantly focus on specific issues related to children in foster care.

What to look out for

- Does the child's functioning or behaviour correspond to what you have been told or what you expected? If not, what is different?
- Don't believe statements like 'it all came out of the blue'. Almost always, there is an explanation and a pattern in a child's behaviour, no matter how covert or delayed their responses may be.
- Observe closely and look for patterns in what may set them off (a request to do something? a request to follow family routines? an attempted interaction from another child? trying to follow instructions or a learning task?).
- What is the child's developmental ability across different domains (physical, cognitive, emotional, social and personal skills; understanding; communication; reading; writing; maths; and so forth)? Remember, it is highly unlikely to be 'all or nothing', that is, their abilities will vary across domains.
- What would you expect for a child of this chronological age across *each* domain?
- Are observed behaviours consistent across situations and environments?
- What appears to work? Why do you think this is?

Exploring and sharing concerns with the child

- Choose the right moment; it rarely works trying to reason in the middle of an argument or outburst. It is best to revisit an incident when everyone is calm, or when it feels right for that particular child. Teenagers can engage more in the car (although there are exceptions when being volatile can be a safety hazard!). You just have to judge and use your intuition.
- The same applies to being gentle, being more direct or making the decision to back off if you are making the child angry.
- What may be obvious to us is not necessarily obvious to them; always try to relate their behaviours to their past history and experiences. A disproportionate reaction to a simple request is not that unusual in an abusive family; this is all that the child knows, and it will take time to rewrite their script.
- Follow the child's clues and what seems important to them.

- Use specific, descriptive and developmentally appropriate words to reflect their behaviour, avoiding judgemental or attributional terms and thus always distinguishing between the child and the behaviour (also see below).
- Establish what the child understands as the behaviour – is their discordance from your or other adults' perceptions?
- Emotional experiences can be more difficult to share, whether because they do not know themselves, do not have the emotional literacy to define, or (usually) simply because they do not trust you, at least not yet. Remind yourself: 'why should they?', rather than feeling hurt and taking it personally. This is typical of children who suffered abuse and neglect, and central to a carer's or professional's competencies that need to be supported by training, supervision and/or simply sharing with their partner, line manager or other support systems.

Now pull all this knowledge together, see if it fits and whether/how to take it further. For a child in care, this is a good time to pass by their social worker. Should you (usually) try to manage within your home or school, work across agencies or seek external help – if so, what do you expect and why? In more complex situations, a multi-agency meeting can help bring clarity and a joint response.

Some management principles

- Balance between nurturing and disciplining.
- As you will need to do both nurturing and disciplining, help the child distinguish between the two, something that may be completely new to them: 'I care for you, but what you did [describe] was wrong, because [spell out why].'
- Be patient; you are not going to change entrenched patterns of behaviours and lifestyles in a short time (something that does *not* reflect on your skills or experience).
- Adopt (and preferably agree) safety measures, but somewhere along the line certain calculated risks need to be taken (such as letting a teenager go out after a period of turmoil); just be clear and transparent with all involved, particularly with the child.
- Be prepared to change task, but never in a panic or in desperation – to do so would only reinforce the child's insecurity that you are not in control.

- Use the behavioural tips discussed in the previous chapter, but run in parallel with relationship (attachment) building strategies.
- Aim for 'sameness' with other children, while bearing in mind that this may not be possible. If a child does not get invitations to parties or sleepovers, or if they cannot cope with other children for very long, plan and structure positive and enjoyable but initially time-limited activities with another child or small group. Share the reasons with other parents, while not labelling the child.
- If there is clear evidence that a child is not ready for a particular approach, make a conscious decision to abandon it before it becomes self-defeating. Replace it with a more pragmatic alternative. Observe the child's progress and try again later. A degree of experimentation is part of normal parenting, schooling and life in general – but is substantially different from 'let's wait and see what happens' or repeating strategies that have clearly not worked before, although nothing has changed since.
- Is your approach consistent with those of other key adults? If not, discuss the reasons with them and establish an easy method of communication and exchange such as through a school diary.

Involving the child throughout

- Use every opportunity to build trust with the child, sharing and discussing what is happening with them.
- Dilute emotive responses or interactions, for example, by using humour, while remaining mindful of not coming across as insensitive or patronising.
- Bear in mind the child's real age across each domain: you may have to treat them accordingly, that is, emotionally as a younger child but intellectually at their chronological age level, or vice versa.
- Share and give something from yourself if you expect the child to do the same. It does not have to be deep-rooted or serious, but it should be a sign of trust building.
- Keep checking that the child understands the tasks. Ideally, the child will agree with the tasks; if they do not have a choice, adopt a clear adult role but explain why that is being done. Avoid shifting between carer mode and friend mode in setting boundaries, as this will confuse the child. Sometimes it is better to have a difficult start rather than a temptingly easy time without clear direction.

- Balance carefully between sensing, listening to and acknowledging the traumatic experiences of the child without becoming a therapist. If the child feels ready to share, disclose or simply cry, take this on, as it may be the first time they have felt able or safe enough to do so. This is different from encouraging or directing 'trauma-related talk' that will leave both child and carer or professional vulnerable.
- Above all, be *genuine* and remain *yourself*! Do not copy others (including tips from this book!) if you do not feel comfortable with their style; instead try to understand why you are feeling uncomfortable. For example, you may be better suited to some types of children or problems, but not for others.

Case scenario

Martin is 15 years old, and he has just come into foster care after an acrimonious two years of intermittently running away from his family, living on the streets or on older friends' sofas. His stepfather hit him a few times when he went back, and he eventually kicked Martin out with an ultimatum to his wife ('it is me or him'). Despite all this, Martin is desperate to go back. He swears at his foster carer when she reminds him to be back by a certain time, telling her that he 'only wants to see his younger brother, as he worries he might also get hurt'. Martin has remained at his school, although he now has to take two buses to get there. He tries to do well, even though he has missed a lot of school and he does not have many friends. Carly, his foster carer, hears him sob his heart out in his room when Martin thinks he is on his own. Carly likes Martin, but she is feeling stuck with so much going on – where does she start?

Some suggestions, although ones that are not necessarily prescriptive in their implementation:

- Getting a sense of the problems, including their hierarchy in terms of risk and severity and their pattern, is a prerequisite to a care plan.
- Some behaviours are probably related to the specific circumstances (family contact and sense of responsibility towards his brother). Other behaviours are probably related to Martin's lifestyle (longstanding lack of boundaries, living in different places, being punished physically). Being a teenager will also come into the equation at times (negotiation on going out, an acceptable time to return home and so forth).
- Different but parallel strategies will be required for each type. For example, arranging regular and supervised contact with his brother in a neutral setting will help reassure

Martin that his brother is well – or, if not, act on child protection grounds; targeting risky behaviours while remaining flexible on others by accepting that Martin cannot quickly conform to consistent boundaries; and constantly seeking positive ways out as for any other teenager, such as by building on positives from his school.

- There should be ongoing communication and negotiation, albeit with clear goals, with Martin and all adults involved.
- Above all, his care status should be clarified as soon as legally or procedurally (for example, parenting assessment) possible, with a clear decision, even if this is unpalatable to Martin in the short term (namely that he will remain in foster care in the long term).

Chapter 5

Young people in residential care

Specific or additional mental health needs

The remit of children's homes and related residential units varies internationally. In many countries, orphanages still operate and care for infants and young children in the absence of care alternatives. In other systems, these can be large settings mixing children as young as six years with teenagers. There are also intermediate provisions, such as the SOS Children's Villages for small groups of children with an allocated carer. As the quality and capacity of fostering and kinship care increase, the trend is for children's homes to look after older adolescents, who almost by definition have not been able to remain with substitute families. This text will largely refer to this group, although most principles and strategies will apply to the other models, too.

In this context, young people in residential care are often (but not necessarily) characterised by:

- previous, often multiple, placement breakdowns
- repeated rejections and secondary difficulties while in the care system
- entrenched behavioural and emotional problems
- longstanding patterns of attachment relationship difficulties with peers and adults
- likelihood of risk-taking behaviours, such as aggression, drug and alcohol use, or unprotected sex
- a range of vulnerabilities to sexual exploitation, bullying, abuse and health conditions
- concurrent externalisation (violence) and internalisation (self-harm) of these risks
- school exclusion and contacts with the judicial system, leading to higher rates of care leavers becoming homeless and replicating the cycle in adult life
- disengagement, with and mistrust of, services.

Young people's needs and residential care systems

One then needs to match those needs and risks with the characteristics of residential units, such as:

- multiple carers
- staff turnover
- difficulties in providing the same boundaries as substitute families
- inversely, attraction to perpetrators who approach young people when most susceptible to cues misinterpreted for affection
- susceptible to peer pressure
- variable and constantly changing staff skills.

Recognition of mental health problems

When contrasting these two levels, one can note the additional difficulties experienced by younger children living with a foster family. Some practical reasons include:

- discrepancy between staff on observations and attitudes, for example, on their connotations of self-harm ranging from 'attention-seeking' to 'a cry for help'
- communication and exchange of information internally as well as with external agencies
- gaps in history, young people's prolonged absences or their reluctance to share their concerns
- the more obvious externalising behaviours masking trauma-related emotional presentations such as depression or posttraumatic stress
- lack of complementary and alternative structured activities at school and in the community to help establish young people's real level of functioning
- the often misleading gap between young people's physical growth and chronological age versus their emotional and social capacity at a younger level
- lack of mental health input when most in need to help staff make these judgements.

Self-reflection

You are the residential key worker of Jenny, a 16-year-old girl who raises a lot of anxiety with her self-cutting, absconding, and verbal attacks on staff and other residents. In-between she can be 'as good as gold', but this does not last. She meets irregularly with a therapist, which she sometimes describes as helpful, while a waste of time when in a bad mood. What concerns you most is that the staff are divided in their perceptions of Jenny and her behaviours. Some think that she is 'manipulative' and 'brings it on herself'. Others speak fondly of Jenny as someone craving affection but being damaged. They tend to agree that there is no pattern in her behaviours, which happen at any time.

Some suggestions

- The staff group need to share these often contradictory views. These may well mirror the girl's past experiences and relationships, hence her unconscious and/or learned (rather than deliberate) trend to split. They may also reflect genuine differences in staff attitudes and knowledge.
- Discrepancies may well also reflect staff dynamics related to the running and ethos of the unit. The leadership by the unit manager, as well as their active facilitation of the staff discussion, is crucial.
- Such discussion, closer observations and regular communication will reveal that behaviours do not happen out of the blue, no matter how sudden they appear. Usually there is a pattern but this may need unpicking, for example, Jenny having a confrontation with one member of staff, and then acting out in a different part of the unit against her peers in what at first looks like an unprovoked incident.

Chapter 6

Adoptive families

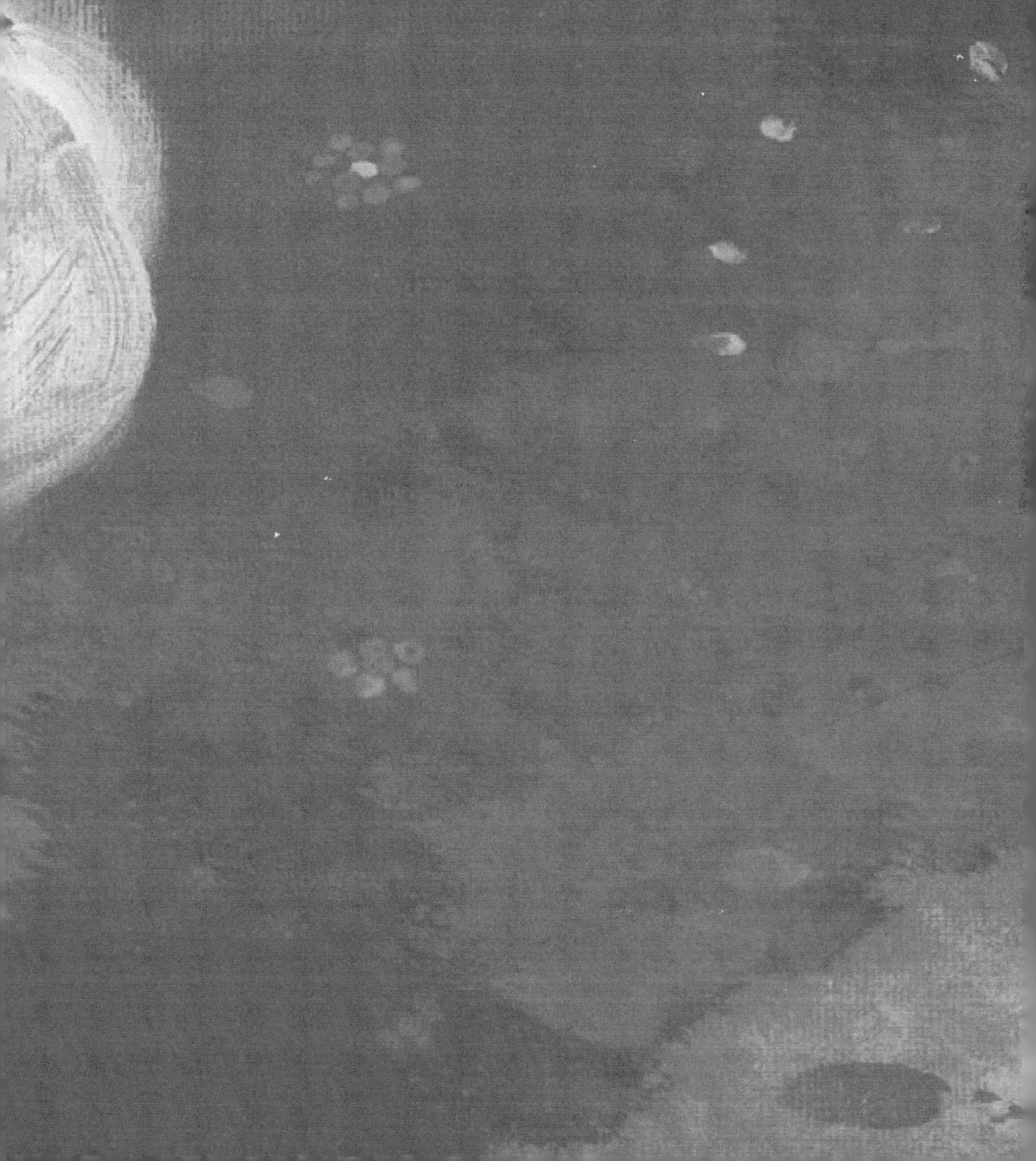

Emotional needs

There are several stages when children's and parents' emotional needs should be taken into consideration, established and met within existing systems, or by drawing on external resources. These obviously have to be placed in the legal and policy context of each country, available supports and families' wishes. Whether they can always be comprehensively and continuously met is debatable, but clarity can help to go a long way as adoption continues to grow across the world.

Parents' decisions and selection process

Procedures in recruiting and selecting adoptive parents and matching their needs with those of children placed for adoption vary by place and constantly change, from being non-existent in some countries (thus relying on adults' simple wishes or decisions to adopt) to well-meaning but over-elaborate and bureaucratic systems in others, with resulting delays and adverse impact on later family life. The problem is that many frameworks remain fragmented, with individual and relational emotional aspects running separately from or in parallel with the legal side, rather than being fully integrated and influencing one another. Consequently, not all the points below will universally apply:

Ultimately, the child's needs are paramount.

- Attitudes, ability to reflect, parenting capacity, life circumstances and placing the child at the centre can be assessed, evidenced and improved in a dynamic, seamless and tight process.
- Training and preparation are equally important for prospective adoptive parents and their assessors alike.
- Skill acquisition cannot be obtained merely from policy guidelines and theoretical knowledge.
- Training and assessment can be intrinsically and sensitively linked.
- Never try to paint a tainted picture of the road ahead; be explicit about the bumps and bruises waiting. Otherwise the pain can be intolerable later.
- If in doubt, it is better to be frank with parents rather than to avoid a difficult discussion, in the hope that their doubts will clear with time.

Defining and establishing informal and formal supports

- Make a pragmatic judgement on the parents' existing networks and resources: are they likely to suffice?
- Acknowledge and anticipate stigma and negative views in the extended family environment or, in some countries, society as a whole.
- Working with family members early on can maximise trust and family support, and thus it can prevent alienation later when the parents may feel the strain.
- Increasing acknowledgement of adoptive families' needs will continue to draw on valuable resources. However, there is often discrepancy between political rhetoric and the reality of what is available on the ground; be frank on the evaluation of resources to avoid managing unrealistic expectations.
- Even where external resources are broadly adequate, over-reliance on these resources can be unhealthy and it may eventually disempower parents.
- Ultimately, no guarantees should be asked for or given on what the child will turn out to be in the future – as indeed no birth ever does offer such guarantees!
- An evaluation of likely external agencies is helpful, in particular on care pathways, remit, and referral criteria.

Preparing the child

The child's needs, chronological and developmental age, timescale and process will vary until the point of (where possible) meeting their adoptive parents. In most Western countries they are likely to be infants or young children, and to be placed in foster care while waiting. In several non-Western countries, adoption can take place directly from an institution. What, when and how a child is told at different stages will depend on these factors. Never promise an outcome that may never be fulfilled, or at a point when the decision is beyond your control. Use developmentally appropriate language, even if this has to convey unavoidable uncertainty. Do not expect an immediate or adult-like response; keep a watchful eye, and do not be surprised if this response comes later or is coloured by verbal or physical aggression. Be prepared to repeat the same simple message calmly, consistently and clearly. All other important adults should be on board to prevent mixed messages that will confuse the child.

Intercountry adoption

- This will be affected by the legislation and procedures of both the country of origin and country of destination.
- Even if it is not mandatory for the country of destination to apply the same policies as for adopting children of their nationality, it is still important to endorse the same standards.
- Additional sociocultural factors need to be taken into consideration, without either minimising or oversimplifying at the expense of core adoption and parenting principles.

Exercise: A placement dilemma

The adoption panel has been debating for two hours whether to go ahead with the placement of Mike, a four-year-old boy, to a recently approved couple in their early thirties. The parents' approval has been relatively smooth. In contrast, Mike has been in foster care for 18 months following severe neglect. He has progressed well, slowly but steadily bridging the gap in most developmental domains. If anything, Mike is becoming clingy and attached to his foster carer, whom he calls 'mummy'. She is becoming attached to him, too. The main reason for not finding a suitable family since Mike was placed for adoption one year ago is that he is of mixed heritage; but it has not been possible to culturally match him with prospective adoptive parents, even after extending the search across several regions. This has, of course, been discussed extensively with Jonathan and Claire, a white middle-class couple, who nevertheless have been consistent that 'it makes no difference' to them.

The panel are split. The parents appear sensitive and clear in their expectations, as well as flexible. Mike is stuck in foster care, getting older and attached to his foster carer. However, Mike's foster carer has been of mixed heritage herself. Will this placement hinder and confuse Mike's identity?

Below are some pointers for consideration rather than a quick answer, as the same scenario may come to a different resolution, depending on these considerations:

- Evidence the advantages and risk of each position.
- Disentangle from personal views or prejudices in either direction.
- Explore concerns, again in an evidenced way.
- Anticipate additional supports and strategies if, for example, the decision is to place Mike with Jonathan and Claire.

- Avoiding a decision by default should not be an option unless a further assessment can be justified, and within a reasonable timescale.

When should we worry?

Besides the usual pointers of concerns about children's mental health at different developmental stages, these will be influenced by these children's characteristics and the adoption process – rightly or wrongly. Either way, one needs to disentangle the facts from the narratives, although even the latter can take a life of their own.

Within the family

- Consider the child's functioning against their chronological age, and across different developmental domains (relationships, personal skills, behavioural, emotional and communication).
- Can any or some of these concerns be explained by their history, for example, of abuse and neglect, and period in care?
- Is there a pattern of improvement and adaptation, albeit slow, if all other factors in the child's life have remained relatively stable?
- Is there agreement or discordance of concerns between the parents or other family members?
- How do these concerns match or contrast with the parents' expectations and preparation?
- How about the 'here-and-now', that is, about parental capacity? If there are concerns in this area, are they related to adoption – for example, uncertainty about how to balance disciplining and nurturing a traumatised child, or are they not relevant, such as not being consistent with boundaries and routines because of their style rather than their perceptions of adoption?

At school and in the community

- A similar consideration of 'past and present' and how these may be related, would be useful.
- Is the child's school level of attainment to be expected in the light of their earlier and recent history?
- What are their relationships with peers like?

- Are there trends of change (improvement or deterioration)? If so, why?
- What are the adult influences and roles – such as from teachers, youth workers and sports coaches? Do they make allowance for the child's needs? Are they overprotective and risk-aversive? Conversely, may they have negative attitudes that impact on the child?

What next?

- Neither panic nor ignore!
- Check that you have considered, explored and discussed the above points.
- Understanding parents' narratives can be as important as facts in guiding the care plan.
- Corroborate with other important informants.
- Do not accept or dismiss anything without investigation.
- Have you consulted with the child, no matter how young, in a safe environment, and taken their views into consideration?
- What has been tried before? If it has not worked (that needs to be established with evidence), why?
- Is there consistency in communication and strategies between the parents and, for example, between them and the school?
- Consider internal resources and informal support systems before going out to other agencies.
- If you need to approach an agency is it one that is appropriate, approximate or by default to the child's and family's needs?
- Make an estimated guess on what they are likely to achieve, including potential limitations because of resources (for example, time-limited intervention) or their remit. Either way, do not raise any false expectations that cannot be fulfilled.

Choosing the appropriate intervention

Several factors will come into play, namely a good formulation of the problem to tackle, availability, skills and children's and parents' wishes. If these do not match, avoid the temptation to opt for a 'default' option, as expectations may not be met, thus resulting in further disengagement. A realistic appraisal on what can be achieved and the sharing of goals will help to prevent this.

- Life-story work can help the child to make sense of their experiences, like putting their life and family puzzle together. This does not extend into interpretations of emotions and working through the trauma as psychodynamic therapy would, but can be a useful prerequisite to it. There can be times when the life story can be repeated at a more developmentally appropriate level or when the child is more settled to utilise it or answer newly articulated questions.
- Behavioural strategies can target specific behavioural or emotional patterns, following the practical tips discussed in Chapter 2. These are not entirely separate from other approaches, but their goals need to be clearly defined, monitored and reviewed.
- Different psychodynamic (in the broad sense, often defined as trauma-processing) interventions can help the child to understand their traumatic experiences and link with their emotions and behaviours. These include their ability to recognise emotions before being able to regulate them.
- Attachment-focused therapies such as theraplay address the above in the context of the parent–child relationship, by involving the parent(s) intermitted or in parallel.
- Family therapy is indicated to tackle communication and relationships difficulties, usually with adolescents – but not necessarily; adoption-related issues may or may not come into the equation.

When is a good time to tell?

It is widely accepted these days that children need to know about their status and history, the question being more about when and how. There are no rigid rules, but some principles include the parents being comfortable with what they share; that they use developmentally appropriate language; that they make a judgement on what information should be shared and how to share it – details on past history or blaming the birth parents will not help the child; and the parents being prepared that this is a process that has to be repeated as the child grows up, with questions being asked at different times and in different ways. It is important that these discussions are initiated in a calm and safe manner, and not in the middle of arguments, so that the child does not associate being adopted with, for example, current home boundaries. A similarly calm approach can be followed regarding requests to look for their birth parents. All of these matters are emotionally powerful, and can feel hurtful and rejecting to the parent as much to the child; thus having opportunities to share and reflect with family members, friends and/or professionals will help the parent to distance themselves and to not reinforce patterns.

Strategies and interventions for universal or frontline practitioners

This is not an exhaustive or even detailed list, but some points for universal or frontline practitioners to consider would be:

- Relate to one's own role.
- Decide (or explore) to what extent one's role is adoption-specific (wholly? largely? partly?).
- As discussed earlier, dealing with a particular problem behaviour is not separate from tackling its underlying causes.
- Agree goals with the family.
- If there are gaps in the plan, because of lack of additional agency involvement, be clear and communicate to the family.
- Adopt a therapeutic framework and adjust to the role.
- Goals should reflect this framework; for example, life-story work may, it is hoped, lead to containment, and hence behavioural improvement, but it is not the treatment of choice for aggression.

Case scenario

Lucy, who is aged 14 years, has been struggling at school for a while, both with her learning and socially. She tended to be rather bubbly, but seems to have gone into her shell lately. Her tutor asked to talk to her, and offered to help if she could. Lucy burst into tears. She shared that she has been miserable and has cut her arms on two occasions, but has not even told her friends. She thought it all started when she visited an adoption social media site. One story was particularly heart-breaking, with a young man deciding to trace his birth mother, only to be told 'my life has moved on, you need to move on, too'. Lucy could not stop thinking about it. Should she try to find out about her birth mother? She thought that she would never forgive herself if she didn't … but then, what if it backfired?

What should Lucy's tutor consider and do next?

Chapter 7

Homeless families and victims of domestic violence

Who are they?

Terms are not universally used for this heterogeneous group. Unlike single homeless young people (see Chapter 8) who are visible and often on the streets, families can typically be found in shelters, other types of hostel settings and a range of community accommodation – whether left to their own devices, such as in 'bed & breakfast' (B&B) or with some support during the period of crisis or through their re-integration to independent living. 'Homelessness' denotes a statutory acceptance that the family have lost their residence on unintentional grounds, predominantly lack of safety, which is a common reason for dispute with housing authorities as economic thresholds constantly change. In reality, the majority of these families are victims of domestic violence, with child abuse and neglect being strong correlates, and therefore it may be easier to understand their needs in this context. Nevertheless, the homeless family population includes fathers as well as multi-problem families who have become homeless for a number of reasons, such as harassing neighbours or perpetrating violence themselves.

Who worries about homeless families?

This invisibility by living on the edges of society and being on the move are key factors in families with the highest level of needs rarely coming into planned contact with agencies, unless they reach an emergency point (for example, for physical or mental health reasons). Mothers are in a state of fear and emotional paralysis, where children's difficulties can neither be easily recognised nor prioritised. Escaping violence and losing their home are understandably paramount, but they are also intrinsically linked with other issues, such as child protection, parenting, child mental health or schooling that, unless addressed, will only perpetuate the cycle. It is worth considering what those needs may be, whatever one's remit of involvement with the family.

Multiple problems and needs

- Hierarchically, safety should be considered first for the mother, children and family as a whole: Are they physically and emotionally safe? Are there child protection concerns, or have there been in the past to one's knowledge?
- The mother's mental health, such as depression or anxiety, and whether it impacts on her parenting capacity, should be considered.

- It is important to consider how the mother's mental health may lead to but also be further impaired by children's behaviours.
- It is important to think about how children may have been affected emotionally by witnessing or experiencing violence and other traumatic events, including those secondary to the moves.
- Adults' and children's physical health status should be taken into account; for example, ask whether children are behind with their immunisations or are underweight.
- Children's developmental ability across different domains should be studied.
- Are they at school following the latest move? What was and is their level of academic attainment?
- Consider their friendships at school and in the community.
- Critically, do the family have relatives or other support networks?

Case scenario

Rosemary is 26 years old. This is the third time she has fled domestic violence in the last two years. She came in the middle of the night after neighbours called the police. She had no time to get any clothes for her or the two children, Chloe (two years old) and Ricky (five years old). Ricky in particular is boisterous, constantly on the go and fearless – he stood up to an older boy at the shelter and later threw a brick at him, narrowly missing him. The children look well cared for, dressed and fed. Chloe rarely speaks; she just follows her mum around and sleeps in her bed at night. Rosemary looks exhausted. She is rather jumpy with people, and she is blaming herself for their predicament. She has talked to the staff about the part of the city she would like to live, but she spends most of the time deep in thought and crying.

As her keyworker at the shelter, you have developed a decent relationship with the family:

1. How would you approach their potential needs across different domains, as described on the previous page?
2. What techniques would you use to elicit information from Rosemary and the children?
3. What other sources may you use to corroborate this information?
4. How would you put all this information in a coherent way to formulate your management plan?

Recognition and assessment

Despite the obvious likelihood of underlying emotional and other mental health problems among both mothers and children, it is far from easy to establish those problems because of families' constant movement, conflicting priorities and potential mistrust. These challenges, nevertheless, also highlight the importance of those in contact with a homeless family critically collating observations, feedback and other information, as this may be the only opportunity for a while to do so, thus preventing further escalation. This knowledge will have to be built up in different ways from previous work based on families in positions of stability, for example, through:

- building trust with the mother and her children
- exploring their concerns and narratives; for example, housing may be more important than mental health at the time
- observing the children around the shelter or in any natural situations, such as during play or activities
- liaising with any available agencies like school, social services or health visiting
- obtaining records, where possible.

Mapping and selecting appropriate agencies

This leads to the importance of good awareness of and networking with other agencies in the area and, if possible, the establishment of joint forums and care pathways for efficient communication, joint working and referral routes. Although homeless families are likely to require a number of agencies because of their complex and multiple needs, in reality most will not be available in a given locality. Crucially, parents may not have the capacity to access services that are not geared to their life circumstances of constant change and fragmentation, and that are likely to vary across localities. Important agencies are:

- statutory or non-governmental organisation (NGO) anti-violence agencies, including police departments
- social care, be it for child protection, family support or advice with benefits
- primary health care, which can be difficult to access for people in transition, and is crucial for rapid entry to the rest of the health system if required, for example, maternity and midwifery services
- health visiting, if there are infants or young children in the household
- adult and child mental health, including for drug and alcohol use, which can also vary in their flexibility with homeless groups

- education, ideally for children to remain in their school but otherwise (such as when they flee violence) a temporary educational placement or support
- non-statutory services related to parenting, mentorship, youth working or leisure activities
- rehousing and related advice.

Ultimately, these agencies will only be efficient if their communication and coordination does not mirror the families' fragmentation. Key working can make all the difference in effectively linking services, particularly if it has an active and therapeutic ethos rather than mere dispersal to other agencies.

Strategies during crisis and early period at the shelter

- Establish current and future risk to mother and children.
- Consider legal or other statutory safeguarding ways.
- Engage mother in safeguarding, including her own protection.
- Establish mother's capacity to utilise existing supports and systems.
- Mobilise protection systems and networks.
- Initiate therapeutic input to mother and children, if available, to contain acute distress and symptoms such as nightmares.
- Ideally bring in mental health practitioners; alternatively, refer externally for acute mental health presentations.
- Engage in parenting work, again prioritising risk-related behaviours. Integrate with practical or creative tasks to enhance engagement.
- Facilitate return to school or alternative provision.
- Arrange creative and leisure activities for the children.

Planning re-integration to the community and prevention

- Assess family needs and match to realistic available resources in the community.
- Identify potential risks for relapse, and discuss with the mother and other important adults.

- Strengthen social and service networks.
- Establish care pathways to new or existing services, and refer appropriately before or after rehousing.
- A keyworker or coordinator can ensure that services remain in place.

Self-reflection

You manage a shelter for victims of domestic violence. Smita fled her home in another city with the support of her sister, and went to the police straight from the train station, who directed her to your service. Smita has a four-year-old daughter, Ananya. Smita has no friends or relatives in your city, and she is adamant that she does not want you to contact any agencies she was previously in contact with, in case she is traced by her ex-partner. She is particularly vocal in not involving social services. All she wants is to 'help to look after Ananya, a house and a school place in a nice area'.

Only one day after coming to the shelter, her key worker asks to talk to you, as she noticed a large bruise on Ananya's leg. When she asked Smita, she initially told her that she had tripped over, and then she started crying, saying that she had not had any sleep, which is why she had slapped Ananya on the leg when she threw a tantrum. She pleads not to tell anyone, as 'this is her only chance'. Then she threatens that she will run off with Ananya if they 'tell the social'. After discussing this with other staff, you realise that they are split between feeling sorry for Smita while worrying about the little girl. They also debate that, should they lose Smita, things may get worse for both mother and daughter.

Some ethical, therapeutic and safeguarding dilemmas

As in many child protection cases, the child's safety is paramount, while wishing to maintain a therapeutic engagement with the mother, who is a victim herself. It is essential to obtain information from social services in the family's previous city on any previous safeguarding concerns as a matter of urgency. Ideally one wants to engage Smita while ascertaining Ananya's safety, before making any further plans. Assuming that the incident and story match, the staff possibly have no option but to report and discuss the incident with the local social services department. At the same time, it is crucial to continue to work closely with Smita to help her realise their wish to support rather than blame her. The possibility of Smita fleeing the shelter is not negligible, in which scenario the police should be alerted. As a manager, you feel for both the family and the staff. You should thus monitor closely and facilitate the staff stance in being supportive while following appropriate procedures.

Chapter 8

Single young homeless people

Common features with other vulnerable groups

It is worth considering the similarities with the 'homeless' aspect of the previously discussed family population, mainly the key principles of relating to and helping homeless people – the parallels with adults living on the streets or in various shelters, and the 'in-between' contradiction of a young mind inside an adult body that suffered awful life experiences and having to fend for themselves. This combination of adopting a developmental and vulnerability perspective is fundamental in helping young homeless people.

Why their characteristics matter so much

- Their characteristics matter so much because they are largely the same group we discussed elsewhere in this book, predominantly care leavers, albeit where circumstances deteriorated so dramatically that they ended up on the streets – whether by being kicked out by their family, running away from abuse or severe arguments or not coping with semi-independent living.
- Their characteristics have to be taken into account as they are likely to have experienced trauma both as children *and* recently.
- We have to consider adult models for young people with a much younger emotional and social functioning capacity.
- We have to consider their multiple mental health, physical health and related needs such as stemming from drug and alcohol use, risk-taking behaviours and particular risks that they are exposed to.

First contact: Think 'homeless' and think 'young'

Both the young person's life context and the practitioner's role – and constraints – will flavour their first contact, assessment of needs and (it is hoped) future help:

a) Someone with a *designated* remit such as a street or shelter worker will have a better chance of aiming beyond that first contact, by:

- building conditions for future trust, rather than expecting trust from the outset

- understanding as many needs as possible at that point, as the young person may be preoccupied with their priorities (for example, housing or specific crisis) and/or be reluctant to open up to others (relationships, emotional distress, drug use)
- make a judgement on what to ask and how far to go; after all, the young person is likely to have seen many people before who asked them the same questions
- use the 'moment' as safely and constructively as possible, bearing in mind that this may still be 'one-off', without guarantees of further contact
- either way, aim to establish a service network for when the young person re-appears somewhere in the system.

b) In contrast, someone in a generic role such as in a health care setting or drug service will be constrained in their time and service engagement 'style'; nevertheless:

- Use as many of the above principles as possible.
- Even a single contact can bring a positive stance through honesty. This should involve dealing with a confrontation in an open and consistent way, for example, a request for drug-prescribing without following through safety arrangements.
- The contact does not end when the young person has left the room; it is important to liaise, corroborate and initiate supports with relevant agencies in anticipation of ongoing unmet needs.

What do young people fear and value?

What is important to us is often not reflected by many young people, especially if they have nowhere to live! This is what studies have found on homeless young people's hierarchies, worries and wishes from services:

- By far the main fear is of alienation and social isolation.
- The next set of fears concern a wish to sort out accommodation, finances and benefits.
- Life skills come next on the wish list, but there is little spontaneous space for physical health and almost none for mental health, unless framed differently and within their broader needs.
- What peers think matters a lot.
- There is typically mistrust of services, particularly concerns about them breaching confidentiality.

- There is frustration with rigid and narrow service criteria and roles.
- There is valuation of caring and supporting staff relationships, flexibility and informal contacts.

Breaking the homelessness cycle

Input from different agencies may well be appropriate and effective for a while. This is often limited by resources or complementary services being available. The 'next best' option is to combine and coordinate what is available in the area for homeless young people as a group, or for individuals if the former is not possible. Ultimately, however, only comprehensive programmes are likely to help young people get out of their predicament and, crucially, equip them sufficiently enough to move on with an independent life. These are the elements that such programmes offer in an integrated model:

- There is initial help to come off the street, but additional continuity for at least six months, if not more.
- There is sustainable accommodation, both in terms of affordability and surrounding supports.
- There is preparation for employment, again with supports to make it sustainable.
- There is risk management.
- There is promotion of physical and mental health.
- There is help to build skills for independent living.

Moving-on stage

The transition to community living should start as early as possibly within the shelter, preferably with sufficient planning and continuity to a wrap-around service that will enhance skills and meet needs in a holistic manner. Some service issues that will help converge rather than fragment this process, are:

- care pathways and agreed protocols with local generic services
- co-location of physical and mental health input or, even better, 'one-stop shops' to cater for all needs and acknowledging that this will become increasingly difficult or desirable as young people settle into their new environment

- dual interventions for mental health and drug and/or alcohol problems
- young person-friendly environments, whether residential or community settings.

Specific applications of mental health interventions

- Specific applications of mental health interventions include goal-directed modalities, be it motivational interviewing, counselling or other frameworks.
- Applications include immediate or short-term objectives, at least to start with, for example, on harm reduction or symptomatic relief.
- Approaches such as CBT, anger management or social skills training can be used but should re-focus to the previous goals, and be combined with other components of skill-acquisition.
- Re-engaging with families, where possible, by setting different goals depending on the circumstances.

Chapter 9

Asylum-seeking and refugee children

Extent of an ever-increasing world challenge

In recent years we have been witnessing an unprecedented global increase of forcibly displaced persons because of persecution, conflict, violence or human rights violations. Approximately 51.2 million individuals fall into this broad group, largely consisting of 33 million internally displaced people, 17 million refugees and 1.2 million asylum-seekers. Conflicts are no longer confined to regions, with the Syrian refugee crisis spreading to Europe, while Syrian refugees have already exceeded 1.5 million in Turkey alone, of whom about 250,000 live in camps. Children under 18 years constitute about 50 per cent of the refugee population, with a total of approximately 25,000 unaccompanied minors applying for asylum annually across 80 countries. Despite variance in response to the refugee crisis between Western countries, and recurrent emotive political debates, which result in different and constantly changing geographical and legal routes, public services are no longer confronted just in selected urban centres but even in remote areas and thus there is the necessity to address needs at policy, service and practice level.

Assessment centres and other early contact points

Many are controversial in their conception and are considered incompatible with human rights, hence the importance of:

- consultation, with the involvement and contribution from child professionals and advocates
- child-centred environments
- staff training in nurturing and not punitive approaches
- consideration of children's rights throughout the asylum-seeking legal process
- incorporation of mental health input adapted to each stage of this process, whether short- or longer-term.

Engagement and recognition of mental health problems

Children's suspicion of authority, their particular sociocultural characteristics and their asylum-seeking situation are all likely to play a part in their state of mental health. It is thus useful to consider:

- how to explain, approach, plan and set up an assessment of their emotional needs
- past experiences on health and welfare services, which will be at best considerably different, if not negligent
- beliefs on mental health and stigma
- language, both literal and conceptual
- that their fear of deportation may flavour their accounts
- that their hope of being granted asylum, particularly if prompted by agents, may flavour their accounts
- physical (somatising) expression of distress
- hierarchy of needs.

Case scenario

You are the support worker of Farshad, a young Afghani man who moved into semi-independent housing three months ago. He said he is 17 years old, but he looks older to you. Farshad keeps to himself, except when being visited by other youth of Afghani origin. He rarely goes out, and is reserved, although polite, when you visit him. Farshad often looks sad, and has gradually started opening up. At the last visit, he burst into tears and recalled his family back home. Then he talked about his father's persecution and eventual murder, before clutching his head in distress. Farhad told you that his headaches are becoming intolerable. He said that he is terrified at the time of going to bed because this is when they get worse. He said that he would like to receive some help but does not trust anyone, as he fears that he may be seen as 'weak' and consequently be sent back to Afghanistan.

How do you approach helping Farhad, both directly and through other agencies?

Making sense of the past and the present

Initial contacts and attempts to share emotional issues are particularly hard. Some practical tips include:

- Check the young person's narrative, expectations, beliefs and worries.
- Beware that the young person's narrative, expectations, beliefs and worries may change and/or be influenced by external factors such as peers and/or legal contacts.
- Remain open on the relevance of past experiences and current adjustment issues.
- Follow the young person's clues and take their concerns (for example, physical symptoms) seriously, even if they cannot as yet make links with psychological factors.
- On the whole, acknowledge awareness of past trauma but do not go into much detail during the assessment phase, unless the young person appears to volunteer relevant information.
- Be prepared to 'back off' if the young person tends to freeze when faced with painful memories.
- Use the young person's terms, followed by prompting to describe what they mean, and give examples.

- Reassure them – only as far as you can – on the boundaries with the legal process.
- Be honest if you cannot offer such reassurance, for example, if you are likely to be asked for a report by the courts.
- You will need to repeat these statements several times, and you may still never eliminate the young person's mistrust.
- Give them the option of being accompanied by a trusted person, at least at the beginning.
- Beware of potential complications if an interpreter is present (see section below).
- Corroborate their narrative with external observations (such as on mood or sleep pattern) with other carers.
- Ultimately, you may need several attempts or 'episodes' before getting through to the young person, or rather them getting through their defences and pain as a first step.

Working through interpreters

Although not automatic for contacts with asylum-seeking and refugee children, it is likely that a substantial proportion will require interpreting input at some point, particularly at the early stages of moving to their host country. This will bring its own challenges, namely:

- interpreters coming from the same community, often being refugees themselves, thus both being important role models and functioning outside their health or social care professional remit; these boundaries need to be clear and monitored
- continuity with the same interpreter as much as possible is important
- training and joint meetings can help improve psychological mindedness beyond technical translation
- that training and joint meetings can help improve psychological mindedness beyond technical translation still applies when dealing with vulnerable children amid disclosures and distress
- resource implications are not negligible and should be anticipated at a service level, rather than on a 'as-you-go' basis.

Specific issues for unaccompanied minors

This is one of the most vulnerable young groups, because of their experiences and status, and for a number of ethical and practice reasons. Systems vary enormously in terms of legal definitions and positioning within the welfare system (in foster or residential care; living independently; treated as children in care or as a distinct group). All these options face their own advantages and limitations:

- Having equivalent status to any child in care offers many safeguards and accompanying supports.
- Having equivalent status to any child in care should, however, be substantive and not tokenistic for economic reasons.
- Foster carers, residential workers and community workers require training in both generic (developmental, safeguarding and mental health) and specific domains (culture and trauma-focused) related to these children.
- Gender and cultural 'mismatches' will need sensitive but firm handling, such as young males being looked after by female foster carers, or being asked to conform to new boundaries and expectations.
- There will be direct access to services such as leisure or other activities, education and health care.

Asylum-seeking and refugee families

Most of the previous issues will apply to parents or families as a whole. In addition:

- Help-seeking may have been initiated by the school or other agency, rather than by the parents.
- Parents may carry their own fear of stigma and/or deportation, thus mistrust of authority.
- These may become particularly pronounced when intermixed with child-protection concerns.
- Cultural differences on what constitute parenting norms need to be handled sensitively, but ultimately they must be in the interests of the child and guided by the host country's safeguarding legislation.
- Parental mental health problems, both in relation to past trauma and persecution and current adversities such as discrimination and unemployment, will require additional attention.

Interventions for asylum-seeking and refugee children

Bear in mind that children may require time to settle into their new life, albeit remaining in limbo about their status and they may thus require more than one attempt before they feel sufficiently safe to engage in trauma-focused psychological work. Some may not be able to do so, at least in the short term or medium term. This does not mean that they cannot be helped, or that different strategies are mutually exclusive:

- Engagement is paramount, taking into consideration other changes in their life circumstances, particularly their legal status.
- Physical complaints need to be taken seriously and be investigated if there are indications.
- Psychological techniques like relaxation therapy can be reassuring in helping young people deal with their physical symptoms.
- Similarly, interventions such as CBT can aim at resilience-building without entering into past experiences if the young people are reluctant as yet.
- A range of trauma-focused interventions have promising emerging evidence with this group, such as narrative exposure, expressive, creative, testimonial, cognitive or eye movement desensitisation and reprocessing therapies, with the aim of re-experiencing and re-creating traumatic experiences.
- Involve carers and professionals in providing consistent responses and in reinforcing the therapeutic goals.

Service issues to consider

- In concentrated areas, direct links should be established between refugee and public services.
- Clear care pathways should be established across organisations.
- There should be consultation and training for community, residential and foster carers.
- There should be outreach work, where appropriate.
- There needs to be clear demarcation from legal services.
- There should be school-based interventions, including in concentrated areas.
- There needs to be mental health awareness among refugee communities.

Self-reflection

You have been seeing Ceynabo, a 16-year-old Somali girl, for counselling for several months, but this has been intermittent and has turned into a frustrating experience. Ceynabo tends to attend every other appointment and begins to engage and share her experiences, in particular being raped before fleeing her village, only to burst into tears and scream that you don't understand her – 'all she needs is some help to sleep'. She will give an excuse for missing the next session, but usually goes into her college tutor's office and asks for help as she cannot concentrate in class. Ceynabo cannot open up or relate to her foster carer and does not have close friends, but she is artistic and dedicated with her school work.

- Ceynabo is clearly ambivalent about counselling, as she finds it painful to delve into her abusive experience.
- This may be a good opportunity to review the therapeutic goals with her.
- She may be amenable to an interpretation of her attitude to counselling, in which case the therapeutic contract could be re-drawn or adjusted.
- In the latter case, or if Ceynabo is not ready to engage, an alternative plan could be to help her with what she defines as her concerns, namely her poor sleep and nightmares, and to revisit trauma-focused work at a later stage.
- A joint meeting with her tutor can help prevent splits and inconsistent responses.
- Avoid mixing therapeutic approaches that mirror the girl's confusion, that is, helping with her symptoms, but share traumatic experiences if and when she comes up with them.
- The above does not preclude from 'therapeutic listening' while reverting to the agreed plan.
- Referring to another therapist or duplicating sessions is more likely to add to Ceynabo's confusion. This should only be initiated if a different therapeutic framework is indicated, and Ceynabo is at least prepared to explore it, rather than offering it by default.

Chapter 10

Young offenders

Specific characteristics of offending youth

It is important to consider three broad themes in addition to other vulnerable and multi-need groups:

- context of policy and setting, that is, how welfare, health and judicial services relate to one another, if at all; and the wider political climate, which tends to swing from reform to punishment, as governments come and go
- continuity between being a victim and becoming a perpetrator
- complex relationship between offending behaviours and mental health.

The latter can be difficult to disentangle, but the following mechanisms are possible:

- Mental illness leads to offending. This is much rarer than public and media perceptions, but can have disproportionate effects.
- Offending behaviours, in the face of trauma, can lead to or exacerbate mental health problems. The most pronounced and worrying vulnerabilities include being bullied and/or becoming suicidal in secure institutions, sometimes with fatal consequences.
- The most common pattern of both offending and ill mental health is underpinned by multiple other problems, both within the family (violence, lack of discipline and nurturing) and the community (school exclusion, peer influences, neighbourhood risks).

Balancing the contradictions of two 'opposite' worlds

A good formulation of a young person's needs in relation to the systemic characteristics of an agency and role are important throughout one's involvement. Goals should be clear, achievable and set within the existing legislative parameters, while remaining mindful of the inherent contradictions between a court sentence and a therapeutic approach. This contradiction will inevitably affect the young person's compliance and engagement, hence likely future success in both domains. Here it is important to stress that this text is not about more specialist forensic input but rather on helping young people who offend, mostly in the community but also in residential settings, in improving their mental health. In that respect, these points will apply to all practitioners in contact with this vulnerable as well as high-risk group.

Factors likely to impact on young people's engagement are:

- being directed by the courts
- nature of their offence and sentence
- previous multiple contacts with agencies and professionals
- parents' presence and attitude
- cognitive capacity
- whether they have sought help themselves
- explanation and preparation.

'It is neither because you're mad, nor bad!'

This message needs to be repeated consistently, in different ways, and by all adults involved. Young people will have their doubts both ways. Their fear of stigma is well documented, but they may also hope that help for their well-being will reduce the severity of their culpability for the offence, and hence have a favourable impact on the court decision. Although this may sometimes be the case, the two pathways should be kept linked but autonomous, as far as possible. The message should thus be that the young person could benefit from help in their own right, and that this would feed into other pieces of restorative, educational or family work they are engaged with, either directly or as a knock-on effect.

As with refugee children and their own prolonged legal process, it is essential that one is honest and does not promise anything that cannot be guaranteed such as that they will not report to the court, even if in the short term this does not enhance engagement. Transparency and consistency are not in many young people's blueprint and, therefore, they may appreciate this approach and know what is mandated by the court and their choices from the outset.

Assessment

- Cognitive and learning capacity can be misleading in a young person not understanding some questions or abstract concepts.
- Behavioural presentations can mask emotional distress, probably more frequently found among young men initially being embarrassed to share their vulnerable side.
- Judge the extent of engagement and adapt interviewing techniques (style, focus and pace) accordingly.

- Observations are equally valid.
- You may decide to restrict first contact to ensuring engagement rather than getting detailed information; vice versa, if the young person is keen to talk, bypass factual information and follow their cues.
- Corroboration from carers and other practitioners, history and existing reports can complement the direct contact with the young person.

The influence of overt or covert risk

This is the most likely youth group to raise anxieties, both in terms of offending and mental health, sometimes in conjunction:

- The most usual mental health concern is harming themselves while living in chaotic and potentially unsafe family or community environments while not engaging with services.
- The rarer but high-risk existence of psychotic illness can also be accentuated by social factors.
- These risks may be interrelated with the current, recent or previous offending behaviours, particularly physical and sexual violence.
- Sometimes covert threats without acting on them (at least so far) can be more alarming, for example, verbal or through drawings implying sexual threat to children or women. The lack of actual offending can make it even more difficult to intervene through formal routes.
- For those reasons, ongoing risk assessment within each agency's remit is essential, followed by regular sharing and monitoring.
- Not explicitly stating a risk because an intervention is not available or likely to work can be as harmful – for example, through over-reacting or impeding other resilience-building approaches like education.

Specificity and adaptation of interventions

Young people's characteristics such as engagement, lifestyle and learning ability will affect the choice and nature of intervention. Goals have to be clear from the outset, that is, whether the target is to reduce and eventually eliminate their offending; to relieve related behaviours and emotional distress; or a combination of those. The less focused these goals are, the less likely they are to succeed. One may accept that trauma re-processing can indirectly lead to less acting out, but not define this as a primary objective, and thus adjust expectations accordingly. Goals must be realistic and shared between the young person, the parents or carers, the professionals involved and the courts.

No therapeutic intervention can be excluded per se, but is likely to require some modification and flexibility. Some particular frameworks have been commonly used with offending youth:

- motivational
- cognitive-behavioural
- interpersonal
- solution-focused
- social-skills training
- range of behavioural strategies.

Service issues

- Service issues should be viewed in the context of the current legislation and policy.
- Services issues are bound to change, depending on predominant political ideologies.
- Primary or universal services aim for prevention of violence and its effects.
- Secondary services target children and youth at risk of perpetrating.
- Tertiary services are for those who have committed offences.
- Ideally, each level should be joined up to mental health interventions, as appropriate.
- Multimodal interventions, integrated services, direct access, and joint-care pathways are more likely to be effective in terms of both engagement and outcomes.

Improving the court process in relation to mental health

- To improve the court process in relation to mental health there should be clarity of roles, processes, links and boundaries.
- There should be joint training involving, for example, magistrates, solicitors, crown prosecution and mental health practitioners.
- There should be protocols.

- There needs to be minimisation of mental health report requests to where directly relevant and necessary, specifying questions for the assessor to address, and thus leading to focused reports.

Case scenario

Greg was back in court after an attack on a young man late at night, when pretty drunk. He was told that 'this is his last chance; otherwise he will get a custodial sentence'. Greg is terrified of 'going down', as he was abused as a child and he panics if placed in the same place with other youth. He still suffers from nightmares, and blames his aggression on the 'voices': 'better get at them first, to keep safe'. Greg is not against getting help, but nothing has worked so far.

Following a mental health assessment that quickly excluded the onset of mental illness but confirmed his vulnerability, parallel interventions were initiated by his youth offending officer and the mental health practitioner on offence prevention and dealing with his traumatic experience. A clear message was given by both of them that Greg would get support and therapeutic input for his 'victim' part, but he had to work hard on his 'perpetrating self' at the same time. Resolving one side would not automatically help the other. This approach was instilled within Greg's education and community activities, and most importantly was routinely communicated to his parents. Slowly but steadily, Greg began to improve on both ends, while comprehending the underlying causes, patterns and consequences of his aggressive outbursts.

Chapter 11

Overarching messages

Therapeutic modalities and evidence-base

The rationale and supporting evidence for different approaches required for vulnerable children who have experienced various types of trauma has been demonstrated throughout this text. While the groups discussed have particular needs, they also share common themes that should underpin the principles behind emerging policy, services and practice. It is acknowledged that not all components will be possible or available, and that countries and systems will vary in their developmental stage. Even where services are relatively well developed, the slightest change in political philosophy and direction will disproportionally impact on these children, as they have multiple needs that cannot easily be met by conventional services.

Policy and legislation

- The more specifically framed is the policy and legislation, the more likely it is to be accompanied by resource allocation.
- Principles and strategies are essential but they should be translated into tangible objectives.
- There should be parallel national and local policy guides and implementation.
- International policy and legislation, including on children's rights, can help less advanced systems to gradually 'catch up'.
- In those circumstances, any one of several domains (physical health, welfare or education) can prove to be the key drive.
- Nevertheless, policy that cuts across all these sectors is the most likely to be effective.

Service planning and development

- There needs to be an acknowledgement that children on the margins, and who are usually the most vulnerable, cannot easily access mainstream services, no matter how high their quality of care.
- Even in the absence of identified resources, it is important that services have clear care pathways, operational criteria and approach to helping traumatised children at different levels, including the associated risks involved.
- There needs to be policy philosophy, interagency care pathways, service commissioning and planning that mirror children's multiple and complex needs in a seamless way.

- There are different service models depending on the extent of need, socioeconomic and geographical factors and available resources; these range between designated teams, posts and approaches within a generic service. The goals and limitations of each model should be clear, and regularly monitored.
- Important service components include integration with welfare systems, direct access, outreach, liaison, consultation and training.

Practice and interventions

- Practice and interventions require a clear framework and evidence-base.
- All existing theories have a place but their indications and goals should be explicit, as should their constraints.
- The particular characteristics of children who experience trauma usually require adaptation of these approaches, or combination with trauma- or attachment-focused interventions.
- Flexibility and innovation are not separate from the evidence-base and theoretical clarity.
- Interventions can be applied at different levels and by various staff, that is, universally, for at-risk children or for those who have developed mental health problems.
- Training and supervision can help maintain boundaries and therapeutic focus in the face of ongoing and overwhelming needs and pressure on staff.

Bibliography

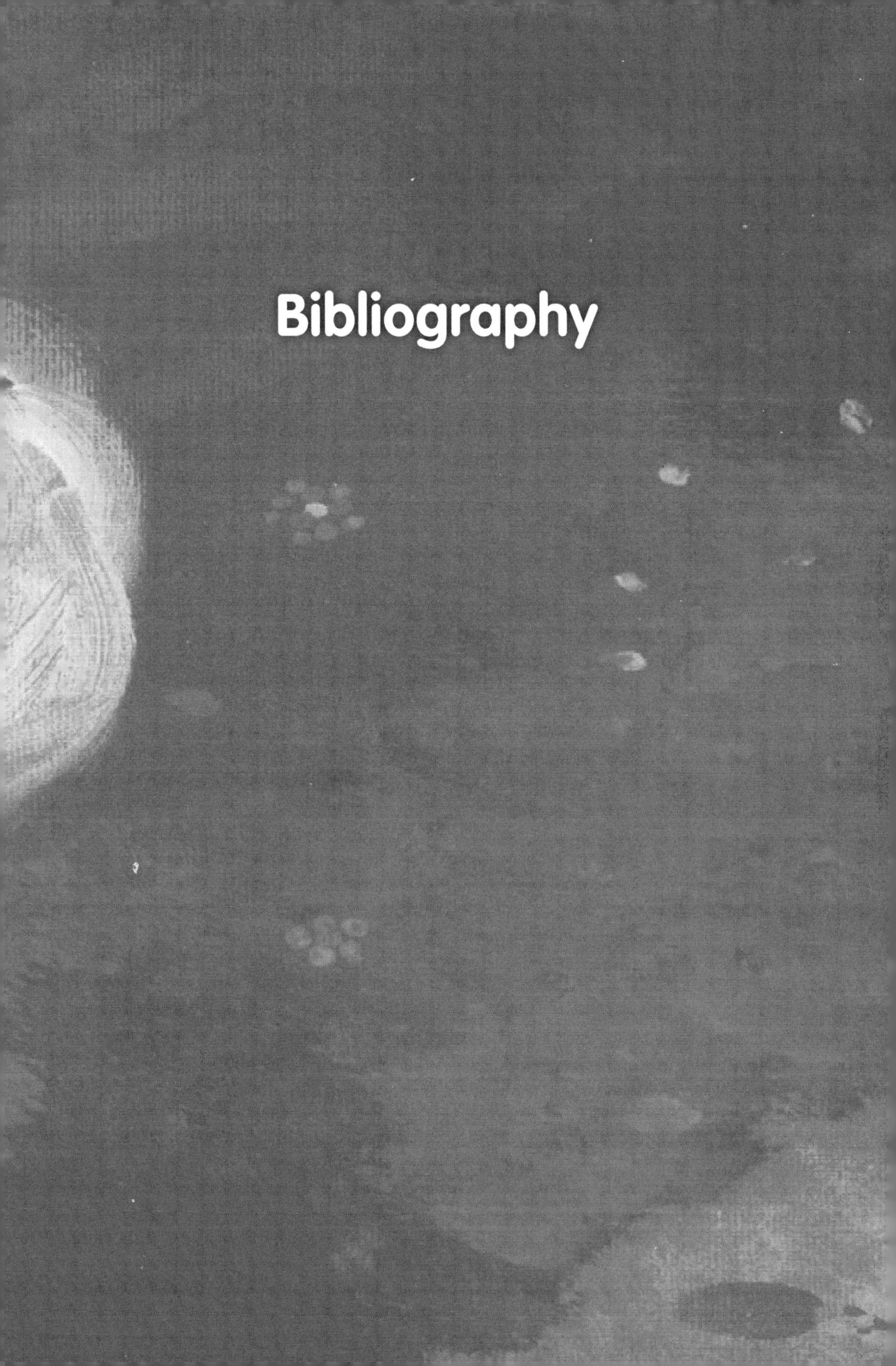

Allen J & Vostanis P (2005) 'The impact of abuse and trauma on the developing child: An evaluation of a training programme for foster carers and supervising social workers', *Adopt Foster*, 29(3), pp68–81.

Altena A, Brilleslijper-Kater S & Wolf JR (2010) 'Effective interventions for homeless youth: A systematic review', *American Journal Preventive Medicine*, 38(6), pp637–45.

Berrick JD & Skivenes M (2012) 'Dimensions of high quality foster care: Parenting Plus', *Children and Youth Services Review*, 34, pp1,956–65.

Betancourt T & Khan K (2008) 'The mental health of children affected by armed conflict: Protective processes and pathways to resilience', *International Review of Psychiatry*, 20, pp317–28.

Betancourt TS, Newnham EA, McBain R & Brennan RT (2013) 'Post-traumatic stress symptoms among former child soldiers in Sierra Leone: Follow-up study', *The British Journal of Psychiatry*, 203, pp196–202.

Betancourt TS, Williams TP, Kellner SE, Gebre-Medhin J, Hann K & Kayiteshonga Y (2012) 'Interrelatedness of child health, protection and well-being: An application of the SAFE model in Rwanda', *Social, Science & Medicine*, 74, pp1,504–11.

Biehal N, Ellison S & Sinclair I (2012) 'Intensive fostering: An independent evaluation of MTFC in an English setting', *Adoption and Fostering*, 36(1), pp13–26.

Bos K, Zeanah C, Fox N, Drury SS, McLaughlin KA & Nelson CA (2011) 'Psychiatric outcomes in young children with a history of institutionalization', *Harvard Review of Psychiatry*, 19(1), pp15–24.

Bowlby J (1969) *Attachment and Loss*, Vol. 1, Hogarth, London.

Bowlby J (1977) 'The making and breaking of affectional bonds: II. Some principles of psychotherapy. The fiftieth Maudsley Lecture', *British Journal of Psychiatry*, 130, pp421–31.

Bowlby J (1988) *A Secure Base: Clinical Attachment of Attachment Theory*, Routledge, Abingdon, Oxon.

Bucher C (2008) 'Toward a needs-based typology of homeless youth', *Journal of Adolescent Health*, 42(6), pp549–54.

Bywater T, Hutchings J, Linck P, Whitaker C, Daley D, Yeo ST & Edwards RT (2011) 'Incredible years parent training support for foster carers in Wales: A multi-centre feasibility study', *Child Care Health Development*, 37(2), pp233–43.

Carnes-Holt K (2012) 'Child–parent relationship therapy for adoptive families', *The Family Journal: Counseling and Therapy for Couples and Families*, 20(4), pp419-26.

Chaffin M, Hanson R, Saunders B, Nicols T, Barnett D, Zeanah C, Berliner L, Egeland B, Newman E, Lyon T, Letourneau E & Miller-Perrin C (2006) 'Report of the APSAC Task Force on attachment theory, reactive attachment disorder, and attachment problems', *Child Maltreat*, 11(1), pp76–89.

American Academy of Child and Adolescent Psychiatry (2010) 'Practice parameters for the assessment and treatment of children with PTSD', *Journal of the American Academy of Child and Adolescent Psychiatry*, 49, pp414–30.

Colonnesi C, Wissink IB, Noom MJ, Asscher JJ, Hoeve M, Stams GJ JM, Polderman N & Kellaert-Knol MG (2012) 'Basic Trust: An attachment-oriented intervention based on mind-mindedness in adoptive families', *Research on Social Work Practice*, 23(2), pp179–88.

De Anstiss H, Ziaian T, Procter N, Warland J & Baghurst P (2009) 'Help-seeking for mental health problems in young refugees: A review of the literature with implications for policy, practice and research', *Transcult Psychiatry*, 46(4), pp584–607.

Dorsey S, Farmer EMZ, Barth RP, Greene KM & Landsverk J (2008) 'Current status and evidence base of training for foster and treatment foster parents', *Children and Youth Services Review*, 30, pp1,403–16.

European Federation of Organizations Working with the Homeless (2010) *Changing Faces: Homelessness among Children, Families and Young People – Autumn 2010*, FEANTSA, Brussels.

Farmer E, Burns B, Wagner H, Murray M & Southerland DG (2010) 'Enhancing "usual practice" treatment foster care: Findings from a randomized trial on improving youth outcomes', *Psychiatric Services*, 61, pp555–61.

Fazel M, Reed R, Panter-Brick C & Stein A (2008) 'Mental disorders among adolescents in juvenile detention and correctional facilities: A systematic review and metaregression analysis of 25 surveys', *Journal of the American Academy of Child and Adolescent Psychiatry*, 47(9), pp1,010–19.

Fazel M, Reed R, Panter-Brick C & Stein A (2012) 'Mental health of displaced and refugee children resettled in high-income countries: Risk and protective factors', *Lancet*, 379(9, 812), pp266–82.

Ferguson L, Follan M, Macinnes M, Furnivall J & Minnis H (2011) 'Residential childcare workers' knowledge of Reactive Attachment Disorder', *Child and Adolescent Mental Health*, 16(2), pp101–9.

Festinger T & Baker AJL (2013) 'The quality of evaluations of foster parent training: An empirical review', *Children and Youth Services Review*, 35, pp2,147–53.

Fisher P & Kim H (2007) 'Intervention effects on foster preschoolers' attachment-related behaviors from a randomized trial', *Prevention Science*, 8(2), pp161–70.

Fonagy P, Gergely G, Jurist EL & Target M (2004) *Affect Regulation, Mentalization, and the Development of the Self*, Karnac, London.

Fonagy P & Target M (1997) 'Attachment and reflective function: Their role in self-organisation', *Development and Psychopathology*, 9(4), pp679–700.

Fonagy P, Target M, Cottrell D, Bevington D & Glaser D & Allison E (2002) *What Works for Whom? A Critical Review of Treatments for Children and Adolescents*, Guilford Press, New York.

Golding K (2004) 'Providing specialist psychological support to foster carers: A consultation model', *Child and Adolescent Mental Health*, 9, pp71–6.

Golding K (2007) 'Developing group-based parent training for foster and adoptive parents', *Adopt Foster*, 31, pp39–48.

Golding K, Dent H, Nissim R & Stott L (2006) *Thinking Psychologically about Children who are Looked After and Adopted: Space for Reflection*, John Wiley & Sons, Chichester.

Green JM, Biehal N, Roberts C, Dixon J, Kay C, Parry E, Rothwell J, Roby A, Kapadia D, Scott S & Sinclair I (2014) 'Multidimensional treatment foster care for adolescents in English care: Randomised trial and observational cohort evaluation', *The British Journal of Psychiatry*, 204, pp214–21.

Gretton HM, Hare RD & Catchpole REH (2004) 'Psychopathy and offending from adolescence to adulthood: A 10-year follow-up', *Journal of Consulting and Clinical Psychology*, 72(4), pp636–45.

Groark C, Sclare I & Raval H (2011) 'Understanding the experiences and emotional needs of unaccompanied asylum-seeking adolescents in the UK', *Clinical Child Psychology and Psychiatry*, 16(3), pp421–42.

Groves S, Backer H, Van Den Bosch W & Miller A (2012) 'Review: Dialectical behaviour therapy with adolescents', *Child Adolescent Mental Health,* 17(2), pp65–75.

Hague G & Mullender A (2006) 'Who listens? The voices of domestic violence survivors in service provision in the United Kingdom', *Violence against Women,* 12(6), pp568–87.

Hanna K (2008) 'Debating war-trauma and post-traumatic stress disorder (PTSD) in an interdisciplinary arena', *Social Science Medicine*, 67(2), pp218–27.

Hodes M, Jagdev D, Chandra N & Cunniff A (2008) 'Risk and resilience for psychological distress among unaccompanied asylum seeking adolescents', *Journal of Child Psychology and Psychiatry*, 49(7), pp723–32.

Hodges J, Steele M, Hillman S, Henderson K & Kanuik J (2003) 'Changes in attachment representations over the first year of adoptive placement: Narratives of maltreated children', *Clinical Child Psychology and Psychiatry,* 8(3), pp351–67.

Holmes B & Silver M (2010) 'Managing behaviour with attachment in mind', *Adopt Foster,* 34, pp65–76.

Howe D (2006) 'Developmental attachment psychotherapy with fostered and adopted children', *Child and Adolescent Mental Health*, 11(3), pp128–34.

Howe D & Fearnley S (2003) 'Disorders of attachment in adopted and fostered children: Recognition and treatment', *Clinical Child Psychology and Psychiatry,* 8(3), pp369–87.

Huemer J, Karnik N, Volkl-Kernstock S, Granditsch E, Dervic K, Friedrich MH & Steiner H (2009) 'Mental health issues in unaccompanied refugee minors', *Child and Adolescent Psychiatry Mental Health*, 3(1), pp1–10.

Hughes DA (2007) *Attachment-Focused Family Therapy,* Norton & Company, New York.

Ingley-Cook G & Dobel-Ober D (2013) 'Innovations in practice: Group work with children who are in care or who are adopted: Lessons learnt', *Child and Adolescent Mental Health,* 18(4), pp251–4.

James AC, Winmill L, Anderson C & Alfoadari K (2011) 'A preliminary study of an extension of a community Dialectic Behaviour Therapy (DBT) Programme to adolescents in the looked after care system', *Child and Adolescent Mental Health*, 16(1), pp9–13.

Jordans M, Tol W, Komproe I & De Jong JVTM (2009) 'Systematic review of evidence and treatment approaches: Psychosocial and mental health care for children in war', *Child and Adolescent Mental Health,* 14(1), pp2–14.

Kerr L & Cossar J (2014) 'Attachment interventions with foster and adoptive parents: A systematic review', *Child Abuse Review*, 23(6), pp426–39.

Keyes M, Sharma A, Elkins I, Iacono WG & McGue M (2008) 'The mental health of US adolescents adopted in infancy', *Archives of Pediatrics and Adolescent Medicine*, 162(5), pp419–25.

Kohrt B (2013) 'Social ecology interventions for post-traumatic stress disorder: What can we learn from child soldiers?', *British Journal of Psychiatry*, 203, pp165–7.

Leathers S (2006) 'Placement disruption and negative placement outcomes among adolescents in long-term foster care: The role of behaviour problems', *Child Abuse and Neglect*, 30(3), pp307–24.

Leathers SJ, Atkins MS, Spielfogel JE, McMeel SL, Wesley JM & Davis R (2009) 'Context-specific mental health services for children in foster care', *Children and Youth Services Review*, 31, pp1,289–97.

Leathers SJ, Spielfogel JE, Gleeson JP & Rolock N (2012) 'Behaviour problems, foster integration, and evidence-based behavioral interventions: What predicts adoption of foster children?', *Children and Youth Services Review*, 34, pp891–9.

Leathers SJ, Spielfogel JE, McMeel LS & Atkins MS (2011) 'Use of parent management training intervention with urban foster parents: A pilot study', *Children and Youth Services Review*, 33, pp1,270–9.

Leve L, Harold G, Chamberlain P, Landsverk J, Fisher P & Vostanis P (2012) 'Children in foster care: Vulnerabilities and evidence-based interventions that promote resilience processes', *Journal of Child Psychology and Psychiatry*, 53, pp1,197–211.

Liberman AF (2003) 'The treatment of attachment disorder in infancy and early childhood: Reflections from clinical intervention with later-adopted foster care children', *Attachment and Human Development*, 5(3), pp279–82.

Littell JH, Popa M & Forsythe B (2005) 'Multisystemic Therapy for social, emotional, and behavioral problems in youth aged 10–17', *The Cochrane Collection*, 4, pp1–36.

Luke N, Sinclair I, Woolgar M & Sebba J (2014) *What Works in Preventing and Treating Poor Mental Health in Looked After Children?*, NSPCC (Impact and Evidence Series), London.

Majumder P, O'Reilly M, Karim K & Vostanis P (2015) '"This doctor, I not trust him, I'm not safe": The perceptions of mental health and services by unaccompanied refugee adolescents', *International Journal of Social Psychiatry*, 61, pp129–36.

McMullen J, O'Callaghan P, Shannon C, Black A & Eakin J (2013) 'Group trauma-focused cognitive-behavioural therapy with former child soldiers and other war-affected boys in the DR Congo: A randomised controlled trial', *Journal of Child Psychology and Psychiatry,* 54(11), pp1,231—41.

Meltzer H, Ford T, Bebbington P & Vostanis P (2012) 'Children who ran away from home: Risks for suicidal behaviour and substance abuse', *Journal of Adolescent Health*, 51(5), pp415–21.

Minnis H, Green J, O'Connor T, Liew A, Glaser D, Taylor E, Follan M, Young D, Barnes J, Gillberg C, Pelosi A, Arthur J, Burston A, Connolly B & Sadiq FA (2009) 'An exploratory study of the association between reactive attachment disorder and attachment narratives in early school-age children', *Journal of Child Psychology and Psychiatry,* 50(8), pp931–42.

Minnis H, Macmillan S, Pritchett R, Young D, Wallace B, Butcher J, Sim F, Baynham K, Davidson C & Gillberg C (2013) 'Prevalence of reactive attachment disorder in a deprived population', *British Journal of Psychiatry*, 202(5), pp342–6.

Mullender A, Hague G, Umme I, Kelly L, Malos E & Regan L (2002) *Children's Perspectives on Domestic Violence*, Sage, London.

Murray L, Cohen J, Ellis B & Mannarino A (2008) 'Cognitive behavioral therapy for symptoms of trauma and traumatic grief in refugee youth', *Child and Adolescent Psychiatric Clinics of North America*, 17(3), pp585–604.

National Institute of Health and Clinical Excellence (NICE) (2010) *Promoting the Quality of Life of Looked-After Children and Young People: NICE Guideline 28,* NICE, London.

Norgate R, Warhurst A, Osborne C & Traill M (2012) 'Social workers' perspectives on the placement instability of looked after children', *Adoption and Fostering*, 36(2), pp4–18.

O'Reilly M, Taylor H & Vostanis P (2009) "Nuts, schiz, psycho": An exploration of young homeless people's perceptions and dilemmas of defining mental health', *Social Science and Medicine*, 68(9), pp1,737–44.

Peltonen K & Punamäki R (2010) 'Preventive interventions among children exposed to trauma of armed conflict: A literature review', *Aggressive Behaviour*, 36(2), pp95–116.

Peterson, PL, Baer JS, Wells EA, Ginzler JA & Garrett SB (2006) 'Short-term effects of a brief motivational intervention to reduce alcohol and drug risk among homeless adolescents', *Psychology of Addictive Behaviors*, 20(3), pp254–64.

Price J, Chamberlain P, Landsverk J, Reid JB, Leve LD & Laurent H (2008) 'Effects of a foster parent training intervention on placement changes of children in foster care', *Child Maltreat.*, 13(1), pp64–75.

Ratnayake A, Bowlay-Williams J & Vostanis P (2014) 'When are attachment difficulties an indication for specialist mental health input?', *Adoption and Fostering*, 38, pp159–70.

Remschmidt H & Walter R (2010) 'The long-term outcome of delinquent children: A 30-year follow-up study', *Journal of Neural Transmission*, 117(5), pp663–77.

Rubin D, O'Reilly A, Luan X & Localio AR (2007) 'The impact of placement stability of behavioral well-being for children in foster care', *Pediatrics*, 119(2), pp336–44.

Rushton A (2003) 'Support for adoptive parents' families: A review of current evidence on problems, needs and effectiveness', *Adopt Foster*, 27, pp41–50.

Rushton A (2007) 'Outcomes of adoption from public care: Research and practice', *Advances in Psychiatric Treatment*, 13, pp305–11.

Rushton A, Monck E, Leese M, McCrone P & Sharac J (2010) 'Enhancing adoptive parenting: A randomized controlled trial', *Clinical Child Psychology and Psychiatry*, 15(4), pp529–42.

Rushton A, Monck E, Leese M, McCrone P & Sharac J (2010) 'Enhancing adoptive parenting: A randomized controlled trial', *Clinical Child Psychology and Psychiatry*, 15(4), pp529–42.

Rutter M (2008) 'Institutional effects on children: Design issues and substantive findings', *Monographs of the Society for Research in Child Development*, 73(3), pp271–8.

Rutter M, Kreppner J & Sonuga-Barke E (2009) 'Attachment insecurity, disinhibited attachment, and attachment disorders: Where do research findings leave the concepts?', *Journal of Child Psychology and Psychiatry*, 50, pp529–43.

Schauer M, Neuner F & Elbert T (2011) *Narrative Exposure Therapy*, Hogrefe Publishing, Ashland, OH.

Selman P (2010) 'Intercounty adoption in Europe 1998–2008: Patterns, trends and issues', *Adopt Foster*, 34(1), pp4–19.

Sinclair I, Wilson K & Gibbs I (2005) *Foster Placements: Why They Succeed and Why They Fail*, Jessica Kingsley, London.

Steel Z, Steel CR & Silove D (2009) 'Human rights and the trauma model: Genuine partners or uneasy allies?', *Journal of Traumatic Stress,* 22(5), pp358–65.

Street E, Hill J & Weltham J (2009) 'Delivering a therapeutic wraparound service for troubled adolescents in care', *Adopt Foster*, 33, pp26–33.

Swann RC & York A (2011) 'THINKSPACE – the creation of a multi-agency consultation group for looked after children', *Clinical Child Psychology and Psychiatry*, 16(1), pp65–71.

Thabet AA, Matar S, Carpintero A, Bankart J & Vostanis P (2011) 'Mental health problems among labour children in the Gaza Strip', *Child: Care, Health and Development*, 37(1), pp89–95.

Thabet AA, Tawahina A, El Sarraj E & Vostanis P (2008) 'Children exposed to political conflict: Implications for health policy', *Harvard Health Policy Review*, 8, pp158–65.

Thabet L, Thabet AA, Hussein S & Vostanis P (2007) 'Mental health problems among orphanage children in the Gaza Strip', *Adopt Foster*, 31(2), pp54–62.

Tischler V, Edwards V & Vostanis P (2009) 'Working therapeutically with mothers who experience the trauma of homelessness', *Counselling and Psychotherapy Research*, 9(1), pp42–6.

Tol WA, Komproe IH, Susanty D, Jordans MJD, Macy RD & De Jong JTVM (2008) 'School-based mental health intervention for children affected by political violence in Indonesia', *The Journal of the American Medical Association,* 300(6), pp655–62.

Tol W, Song S & Jordans M (2013) 'Resilience and mental health in children and adolescents living in areas of armed conflict: A systematic review of findings in low- and middle-income countries', *Journal of Child Psychology and Psychiatry*, 54(4), pp445–60.

Toth SL & Gravener J (2012) 'Review: Bridging research and practice: Relational interventions for maltreated children', *Child and Adolescent Mental Health,* 17(3), pp131–8.

Tucker DJ & MacKenzie MJ (2012) 'Attachment theory and change processes in foster care', *Children and Youth Services Review*, 34, pp2,208–19.

United Nations Children's Fund (UNICEF) (1989) *Convention on the Rights of the Child,* General Assembly, New York, www.unicef.org.uk/UNICEFs-Work/Our-mission/UN-Convention (accessed 29 October 2015).

Vostanis P (ed.) (2007) *Mental Health Interventions and Services for Vulnerable Children and Young People*, Jessica Kingsley, London.

Vostanis P (2014a) (Editorial) 'Meeting the mental health needs of refugee and asylum seekers', *British Journal of Psychiatry*, 204, pp176–7.

Vostanis P (2014b) *Helping Children and Young People who Experience Trauma: Children of Despair, Children of Hope*, Radcliffe, London.

Vostanis P (*in pressa*) 'New approaches to interventions for refugee children', *World Psychiatry.*

Vostanis, P (in pressb) (Editorial) 'The impact of war on caring professionals', *Journal of Psychiatric and Mental Health Nursing.*

Ward H, Munro E, Dearden C & Nicholson D (2003) *Outcomes for Looked After Children: Life Pathways and Decision-making for Very Young Children in Care or Accommodation*, Department for Education and Skills, London.

Westermark P, Hansson K & Olsson M (2010) 'Multidimensional treatment foster care (MTFC): Results from an independent replication', *Journal of Family Therapy*, 33, pp20–41.

Zeanah C, Berlin LJ & Boris NW (2011) 'Clinical applications of attachment theory and research for infants and young children', *Journal of Child Psychology and Psychiatry*, 52(8), pp819–33.

Zeanah C, Egger H, Smyke A, Nelson CA, Fox NA, Marshall PJ & Gurthrie D (2009) 'Institutional rearing and psychiatric disorders in Romanian children', *American Journal of Psychiatry*, 166(7), pp777–85.

Zeanah C, Larrieu J, Heller S, Valliere J, Hinshaw-Fuselier S, Aoki Y & Drilling M (2001) 'Evaluation of a preventive intervention for maltreated infants and toddlers in foster care', *American Academy of Child and Adolescent Psychiatry*, 40(2), pp214–21.